"I'm experiencing tiredness, a change in weight, and apathy toward things I used to enjoy . . .

. . . DO I NEED PROFESSIONAL HELP?"

Psychological Symptoms is your essential guide to the spectrum of psychological conditions, and their symptoms and treatment. You'll find answers to such vital questions as . . .

- Would I know if my teenager was suicidal?

- What are the telltale signs of eating disorders?

- Is depression an inevitable part of aging?

- How effective is group therapy?

- Who should I select for my treatment—a psychologist or a psychiatrist?

- What are the risks and benefits of antianxiety medications?

- Can I be sure my therapist is right for me?

- Are men or women more prone to manic depression?

- Can passive-aggressive behavior be curbed with medication?

. . . AND MUCH MORE

D0452025

The Berkley Total Health Series

HIGH TIMES/LOW TIMES: HOW TO COPE WITH TEENAGE DEPRESSION

LIGHT UP YOUR BLUES: A GUIDE TO OVERCOMING SEASONAL DEPRESSION AND FATIGUE

NEW MEDICINES OF THE MIND: A UNIQUE CONSUMER GUIDE TO TODAY'S PRESCRIPTION DRUGS

COMMON AND UNCOMMON SCHOOL PROBLEMS: A PARENT'S GUIDE

PSYCHOLOGICAL SYMPTOMS: A CONSUMER'S GUIDE TO DIAGNOSIS AND AVAILABLE TREATMENTS

PSYCHOLOGICAL SYMPTOMS:
A CONSUMER'S GUIDE TO DIAGNOSIS AND AVAILABLE TREATMENTS

MARK A. GOULD, M.D.

B

BERKLEY BOOKS, NEW YORK

This book is not intended to replace personal medical care and supervision; there is no substitute for the experience and information that your doctor can provide. Rather, it is our hope that this book will provide additional information to help people understand the nature of psychiatric disorders and diagnoses.

Proper medical care should always be tailored to the individual patient. If you read something in this book that seems to conflict with your doctor's instructions, contact your doctor. Since each individual case differs, there may be good reasons for individual treatment to differ from the information presented in this book.

If you have any questions about any treatment in this book, consult your doctor.

In addition, the patient names and cases used in this book do not represent actual people, but are composite cases drawn from several sources.

This Berkley book contains the complete text
of the original edition. It was completely
reset in a typeface designed for easy reading,
and was printed from new film.

PSYCHOLOGICAL SYMPTOMS

A Berkley Book / published by arrangement with
PIA Specialty Press, Inc.

PRINTING HISTORY
PIA Press edition published 1989
Berkley edition / June 1990

A BERKLEY BOOK® TM 757,375
Berkley Books are published by The Berkley Publishing Group,
200 Madison Avenue, New York, New York 10016.
The name "BERKLEY" and the "B" logo
are trademarks belonging to Berkley Publishing Corporation.

PRINTED IN THE UNITED STATES OF AMERICA

10 9 8 7 6 5 4 3 2 1

DEDICATION

To my wife, Gloria, and our two sons,
who through their love
have been of consistent support and understanding.

ACKNOWLEDGMENT

I wish to express my appreciation to all the patients I have been privileged to see through my professional career. They have taught me about their pain and how to be of help to them.

I would also like to acknowledge the many excellent Brawner professionals, at all levels, with whom I have had the privilege to be associated during my professional career.

In addition, I am also genuinely appreciative of the significant efforts of Marilyn Devroye, Ron Schaumburg, Bonnie Redlich, and Elza Dinwiddie-Boyd, whose obvious talents have contributed to the creation of this book.

TABLE OF CONTENTS

SECTION I

INTRODUCTION   3
1. Opening the Door   9
2. Children, Teenagers, and the Elderly   24
3. Psychiatric Medications   37
4. Inpatients, Outpatients, and the
   Different Types of Treatment   51
5. Evaluating Your Treatment   64

SECTION II: COMMON PSYCHIATRIC DIAGNOSES

6. Disorders That May First Appear in Infancy,
   Childhood, or Adolescence
   - Autistic Disorder   77
   - Mental Retardation   80
   - Attention-deficit Hyperactivity
     Disorder   82
   - Conduct Disorder   85
   - Oppositional Defiant Disorder   87
   - Anorexia Nervosa   88
   - Bulimia Nervosa   90
7. Organic Mental Disorders
   - Organic Mental Disorders
     (general information)   94

Primary Degenerative Dementia
   of the Alzheimer Type   95
Psychoactive Substance-Induced
   Organic Mental Disorder   97
8. Anxiety Disorders
   Panic Disorder   99
   Panic Disorder With Agoraphobia   102
   Social Phobia   104
   Simple Phobia   106
   Obsessive Compulsive Disorder   107
   Posttraumatic Stress Disorder   109
   Generalized Anxiety Disorder   111
9. Mood Disorders
   Bipolar Disorder   113
   Major Depression   115
   Dysthymia   118
10. Sleep Disorders
   Insomnia Disorders   121
   Hypersomnia Disorders   123
   Sleep-Wake Schedule Disorders   125
   Parasomnias
      Dream Anxiety Disorder
      (Nightmares)   127
   Sleep Terror Disorder   129
   Sleepwalking (Somnambulism)   131
11. Schizophrenia   133
12. Personality Disorders
   Antisocial Personality Disorder   138
   Avoidant Personality Disorder   140
   Borderline Personality Disorder   141
   Dependent Personality Disorder   143
   Histrionic (or Hysterical)
      Personality Disorder   144
   Narcissistic Personality Disorder   145
   Obsessive Compulsive Personality
      Disorder   146
   Paranoid Personality Disorder   148

Passive-Aggressive Personality
  Disorder   149
Schizoid Personality Disorder   150
Schizotypal Personality Disorder   152
13. Other Disorders
  Delusional (Paranoid) Disorder   154
  Adjustment Disorder   157
14. Alcohol and Substance Abuse
  Alcohol Dependence (Alcoholism)   160
  Psychoactive Drug Dependence
    or Addiction   162

SOURCES   165
INDEX   167

PSYCHOLOGICAL SYMPTOMS:
A CONSUMER'S GUIDE TO DIAGNOSIS AND AVAILABLE TREATMENTS

SECTION I

INTRODUCTION

When the pain of psychiatric disability first occurs, you become aware that emotional pain can hurt just as much as physical pain. It doesn't really matter where it comes from—you simply want the pain to stop. Whether it is you yourself or someone you love who is affected—and whether the disability is depression, anxiety, an eating disorder, or substance abuse—what really matters is that something isn't right and you need help.

Suddenly, a different world confronts you. This is a strange and new world using a strange and confusing vocabulary. Terms such as affective illness, bipolar disorder, personality disorder, chemical dependency, and attention-deficit disorder are just a few of the medical phrases that will now become part of your everyday thoughts. You have dozens of questions in mind, which are complicated by the vestiges of shame and guilt left over from centuries of ignorance about psychiatric illness and the stigma that still lingers. "Why do I feel this way?" "What did I do wrong?" and "Why does he act that way?" are a few of the frequent, and difficult, questions that emerge.

As medical director of Brawner Psychiatric Institute, I've

heard all of these questions and more. But there are two questions that dominate: "Where do I go for help?" and "which one of the many treatments available is the right one for me?"

Regrettably, some people never find the answers. Even worse, some people never stop to ask these important questions. Instead, they struggle to survive without help—a struggle they may not win. Often they refuse to seek help because of the stigma associated with psychiatric disorders, or because of the guilt associated with mental health problems. "If only I had more willpower," laments the addict. "If only I could pull myself together, then I'd feel better," sighs the depressed woman. "If only I was a better parent," says the mother of a child with attention-deficit disorder.

These types of thoughts, with their accompanying concept of "moral weakness," are not unusual. Unfortunately, they may interfere with seeking appropriate and effective treatment for these established medical disease symptom complexes.

Initially, it is not unusual to have such thoughts. After all, it is quite natural and human to have doubts about yourself. But these thoughts should never interfere with getting the proper help and treatment for a psychiatric disorder. Psychiatric disorders do not reflect a weak-willed individual, or a flaw in the individual's moral character. Rather, these psychiatric conditions are frequently based on physiological causes, and are usually treatable disease entities.

Over the past several years, I have noted—and been surprised by—the large number of patients who fail to seek appropriate treatment in a timely way. The decision to reach out for help is postponed until a late stage of the development of the illness. Postponement of treatment is unfortunate, for it frequently leads to the necessity of hospitalization, legal intervention, an extended period of recovery—and even irreversible changes. Death itself, as a result of suicide or homicide, may be the outcome in some types of illnesses.

In asking myself why this large population group has not sought help, I've concluded that there are certain underlying reasons:

1. Lack of understanding about the symptoms of mental illness
2. A fear of the unknown related to psychiatric treatment
3. Lack of awareness of how to enter the mental health treatment system when that is indicated

I hope this book may help with these problems.

Today, doctors and researchers have discovered the physiological nature of a wide range of psychiatric disorders—addiction, anxiety disorders, manic-depressive disorders. Although we may not always know the exact cause of an illness, we frequently know which medicine or other treatment intervention is likely to help. This really isn't very different from other medical problems, such as diabetes, cancer, and the common cold. We don't fully understand the originating cause of these diseases but nevertheless have some excellent ideas about specific interventions to relieve symptoms or prevent the advance of the disease.

Some people do seek help for psychiatric disease, but without carefully considering the source. They may select a therapist because "she helped that friend of Aunt Sally's," or pick a psychiatrist out of the phone book, or call a therapist identified on a talk show. They make their choice without considering the background or training of the therapist, and without understanding either the course of treatment or its goals. In getting help, it is important to consider the type of illness and what the options for treatment of that illness might be, before you can make a rational choice about a therapist. In this book, I suggest a few steps that might be of help in making that rational choice. However, I don't want you to subject yourself to unnecessary steps that might interfere with getting help promptly.

Delving into treatment without a basic knowledge of the psychiatric disorder and its treatment process can be likened to needing an automobile but going to a bicycle salesman. The bicycle salesman simply does not have what you need, and although you might leave with a form of transportation, the ride isn't what you expected or needed. Unfortunately, this scenario characterizes how many people approach initial treatment decisions.

If you are like the majority of people, you know very little about psychiatry. When does an illness require the services of a psychiatrist? Can another type of mental health professional provide appropriate treatment? Unless you have a ready resource of expertise, such as an informed family doctor, to help you answer these questions, you may find yourself floundering as you try to make the best decision. Unfortunately, the burden of your symptoms, or the pain experienced by your family system, may interfere with the quality level of your decision. You need, and hopefully want, the best help available. My personal philosophy is that I welcome help anytime someone wishes to do so, and I hope you will let others help, too. I hope this book will be of help to you!

Modern psychiatry now uses improved diagnostic technologies and procedures, as well as revolutionary therapeutic tools that were simply not available just a few years ago. The development of successful psychiatric medications over the past thirty-five years has been significant, and has revolutionized the treatment of previously resistant disorders.

Some of you may not remember, but in the 1950s, before the advent of many of these medications, America faced a major crisis: what to do with the burgeoning mentally ill population. Our psychiatric institutions were overflowing with patients. Dire forecasts were made of an America that would soon be overwhelmed by mental illness. However, advancements in psychiatry have led to the discovery of an entirely new class of drugs, which have changed the face of treatment possibilities. Today, because of this revolution, there are many fewer chronically institutionalized patients than there were in 1955.

In an age when most psychiatric disorders can be successfully treated on an outpatient basis—an age where hospital stays are short and where scientists demonstrate every day the inextricable relationship between biological and psychological functioning—you and your family member should be encouraged that you have many more treatment alternatives at your disposal than ever before. You must seize the opportunity to make the best choice from this wide spectrum of possibilities. In order to make the right decision, you need to be informed and not handicapped by feelings of guilt or stigmatization.

Not only do we have more effective medications, but our understanding of proper dosage, length of therapy, potential for side effects, and ways to minimize side effects has grown immensely, expanding tremendously in the thirty years of my professional career. This sophistication and increased specificity has refined psychiatric practice; we have learned a great deal and will continue to learn a great deal more in the future.

Biological or physical factors lie at the root of a great number of psychiatric conditions, including alcoholism, depression, manic-depressive disorders, schizophrenia, and panic attacks. Awareness of this is relatively new. It does not mean that environmental factors are not also important; however, with the presence of the biological factor, a given patient may be more vulnerable to a given environmental stress.

Let me give you a nonpsychiatric example of which we are all aware. It is now well known that elevated cholesterol levels contribute to premature hardening of the arteries. Those individuals who have a genetic predisposition of difficulty in metabolizing cholesterol frequently can forestall hardening of the arteries with careful dietary habits and—sometimes—with special medications. On the other hand, a person who does not have the cholesterol metabolism defect does not experience the same need to restrict his diet. Eating ice cream is not a problem for the individual without the genetic predisposition, whereas it is a very real threat to the patient with the genetically inherited metabolism difficulty. And so it goes with mental illness. Environmental factors and stress are a threat to some who are predisposed to the development of certain types of psychiatric illnesses. These individuals will, we hope, learn to live around the environmental stress. On the other hand, the same stress may present no problem at all to people without the predisposition.

• • •

Today's psychiatrists have been trained to treat both the medical and psychological needs of patients. Thus the world of psychiatry holds great promise for doctor and patient alike. I want this book to be your guide to that world.

1

OPENING THE DOOR

The first step—the one in which you decide to seek treatment—is extremely significant and important. That decision itself is frequently accompanied by a sense of encouragement now that you have decided to move ahead. What now?

It may be confusing when you learn that there are many different types of therapists, different types of treatment philosophies, and various schools of thought. Will the treatment provider be a psychiatrist, a psychologist, or some other mental health professional? Will the type of therapy be oriented around psychodynamic principles, behavior therapy, or other? How can you tell the difference? And just what do these terms mean anyway?

.It will help if you have the resource of a trusted expert who can help you through this maze. Unfortunately, this type of resource is not always readily available.

There are some basic differences in the training and skills possessed by different mental health professionals.

What Is a Psychiatrist?

A psychiatrist is a doctor of medicine who has attended four years of medical school and then completed a psychiatric residency of four years' duration in preparation for understanding and treating mental disorders. The psychiatrist is trained in medicine. This is the one mental health professional who can consistently consider the impact of physical factors on the psychiatric symptom complex. This is the mental health professional who can outline a medical workup, including physical examination, appropriate laboratory studies, and follow up with the prescription of medications, if indicated.

What Is a Psychologist?

The Ph.D. psychologist is a mental health professional who has specifically studied psychological illness in a graduate education program following college education. This professional becomes quite proficient in the diagnosis of psychological illness, in performing psychological testing and evaluation, and in some very specific and helpful nonmedical treatment interventions. The focus of education of the psychologist is not on medical science and human illness, but rather on understanding human behavior.

Other Mental Health Professionals

There are other mental health professionals who may be trained as social workers, counselors, or other. They may be quite proficient at special types of "talk therapy" because of their special interests and/or training.

Many of you may not know how to choose between the multitude of mental health professionals who are now available. There is an extensive array of accrediting and certification organizations, which result in a list of initials after the professional's name. Sometimes, these "certifications" are confusing.

When in doubt—when a special, trusted expert is not available for guidance—I would seek out a psychiatrist and request an evaluation and recommendations for treatment options. You should not hesitate to question whether alternative therapists are available and appropriate for the type of illness presented. The reason I recommend a psychiatrist at this level of the decision-making process is simply that the psychiatrist is a doctor specializing in emotional illness, fully trained in the medical sciences.

Like a cardiologist or gynecologist, a psychiatrist is a medical specialist. Some people find this hard to believe, arguing that the mind has no direct relationship with the body. In reality, however, your mind, and your thoughts, are inextricably bound to your body and brain. There is a wondrous, complex, and intricate relationship between mind and body. The psychiatrist is the mental health professional who can treat both the mind and body, mentally and physically. The psychiatrist can outline and order medical evaluation when that seems appropriate, and prescribe necessary medication.

It is now accepted that mental illness cannot be satisfactorily understood by considering only psychological and social factors. Understanding mental illness requires an appreciation of the total person, including medical, psychological, and social factors: abnormalities in brain structure; alterations in neurotransmittors; disorders of the endocrine, cardiovascular, or central nervous system; and toxic metabolic factors caused by blood chemistry changes.

Thus, an accurate diagnosis requires careful evaluation of all of the conditions that may affect the patient.

I am sure you understand why it is so very important not to underestimate the medical basis of psychiatry. Through the years scientific research has consistently revealed the biological foundation for symptoms that appear as psychological problems. As an example, up to 40 percent of the diagnoses of depression represent a misdiagnosis of a physical illness.

Consider, also, a "psychiatric disorder" that plagued the South for decades. At one time, countless individuals were hospitalized with symptoms of anxiety, depression, and dementia. Often, these individuals were troubled by headaches, insomnia, and memory lapses—all apparently psychiatric problems. In reality, however, these individuals were suffering from *pellagra*—a condition caused by a vitamin (niacin) deficiency. For years, pellagra was a very common problem in the United States, but especially in the South, where a diet based on corn, fatback, and molasses—all deficient in niacin—often caused pellagra. At that time, approximately 50 percent of state mental institution hospitalized patients were really suffering from a niacin deficiency! Since science discovered the niacin factor in 1937, the vitamin has been added to many cereal products, including bread, greatly reducing the number of hospitalized patients.

In a similar way, many other medical problems may present themselves with psychological symptoms. To name but a few, hyperthyroidism, disturbances of the adrenal glands, brain tumors, and lupus erythematosus all show psychological symptoms.

On the other side of this issue, we see a large group of disorders known as psychogenic. These problems appear as physical symptoms, but really represent an underlying emotional disorder. Many of you will recognize the relationship of stress/tension to development of physical symptoms. Complaints such as "you give me a headache," "that makes me sick to my stomach," or "what a pain in the neck" are old expressions but obviously insightful, as they recognize the relationship between body and mind.

At this point in time, psychiatric research continues to uncover further biological explanations for many mental disorders. We know, for example, that panic attacks—once considered a purely psychological problem—are really in part caused by malfunctions in specific areas of the brain. Other psychiatric symptoms may actually be caused by biochemical imbalances of the substances that regulate our moods. Exactly what causes panic attacks or some other psychiatric disorders has not yet been fully determined. Nevertheless, we do have some idea of the physical factors, and effective treatment interventions based on these are now available.

The sophistication of current lab studies has brought the psychiatrist and neurologist much closer together, as both are seeking and identifying specific areas of the brain that are responsible for specific symptom complexes. As these discoveries are made, development of specific treatments is refined. The future is bright—and that is important to remember.

Unfortunately, misdiagnosis can occur if, as I mentioned before, a careful medical evaluation is not carried out. The delay that results from misdiagnosis only serves to compound the pain that the patient experiences. Let me tell you about a former patient of mine.

Jane had seen several psychotherapists because of symptoms of depression over a twelve-year period of time. She had had several different types of therapy and also had taken antidepressant medications. Although she did gain an increased level of understanding about herself, the symptoms recurred and she still felt depressed.

When Jane first saw me she said, jokingly, "I feel like that Woody Allen character in *Annie Hall*. You know, when he said, 'fifteen years of therapy—I'm going to give it one more year and then try Lourdes.' Well, you are my last stop before Lourdes."

But Jane's problem was no laughing matter. She described symptoms of depression, feelings of uselessness and hopelessness, and how she would suddenly burst into tears for no reason. She also described feeling a strange tightness in her chest, and an odd inability to wear turtlenecks or any clothing with a tight collar. She shared this with me in an offhand manner, as if merely describing one of many symptoms with which she struggled. But this particular symptom represented an important revelation.

We scheduled a physical examination and laboratory tests to evaluate the way her thyroid gland functioned. Fortunately, we determined that Jane had a malfunctioning thyroid, which was very easy to correct by taking supplemental thyroid hormone. Jane's years of therapy had failed to uncover this because her therapists did not have the necessary medical background and were therefore not prepared to think about thyroid disorder as a possible cause for the depression. In fact, thyroid disorder is a common problem that may occur in 10 to 15 percent of depressed individuals.

Although Jane needed more psychotherapy, it was on a short-term basis. Unfortunately, there is no medication that can replace the twelve years of struggle characterized by destructive thoughts and attitudes. However, we were soon able to help Jane improve her self-image, and to understand how her past actions had been influenced by the thyroid disorder. On this occasion, her psychotherapy was of less than four months' duration.

Given a proper and thorough diagnostic approach, psychiatry can identify the so-called "medical mimickers": physical diseases that masquerade as disorders of the mind. Improvements in diagnostic techniques and procedures have helped many psychiatric patients avoid unnecessary suffering.

But modern psychiatry is more than improved diagnosis. Today, psychiatrists have at their disposal safe, effective medications, which are discussed in subsequent chapters. The remainder of this chapter, however, will focus on the different types of psychotherapy, and how they may be used by the psychiatrist, psychologist, or other mental health professionals.

The Role of Psychotherapy and Psychotherapists

I have already strongly emphasized my firm belief of how important a medical background is in initial evaluation and planning of treatment. This emphasis on medicine does not mean that the practice of psychiatry is purely biological. It is not. The art and science of psychology provide the tools for the psychiatrist to practice psychotherapy. After identifying and treating the biological root of a disorder, the patient may still continue to need psychotherapy. A successful intervention with medication will relieve symptoms, and in many instances prepare the patient to make much better use of psychotherapy. Frequently, the length of time in psychotherapy is shortened.

Psychotherapy can be defined as the treatment of mental and emotional disorders based on verbal and nonverbal communications with the patient. This definition encompasses a broad range of therapies. Although many kinds of psychotherapy are practiced today, I want to discuss just a few of the more common types that a patient might encounter.

I have often thought that engaging in psychotherapy was much like going on an African safari. The therapist is the guide and you are the one on safari. It is your trip, and how much you get out of it largely depends on you. The therapist functions as someone who has been over this kind of trip before and has the expertise to point out to you some of the hazards that he or she has learned to recognize. Plus, the therapist has the ability to make suggestions that might help you choose less hazardous alternatives.

The information given here is not sufficient to let you decide which of these specific therapies you need. Rather, it is my intention to help you understand some of the treatment recommendations that might be made to you, so that you can discuss these and inquire about them with your therapist. Again, I recommend an initial consultation with a psychiatrist—a medically trained mental health professional—so that an accurate diagnosis can be established. That diagnosis is extremely important, so that your doctor can make a decision about the most appropriate type of treatment for you.

Which Door to Open? The Different Types of Psychotherapy

There are many different schools of thought regarding psychological treatment. Frequently, there are very specific indications for different therapies. Your doctor should explain this to you and direct you to the specific type of therapy that is most appropriate for your disability.

"Analysis" is a term that is frequently thrown about loosely, but psychoanalysis represents a very sophisticated, time-consuming, and potentially expensive treatment modality. There are specific indications for psychoanalysis, and you should have very competent consultation when seeking advice about it. It is not for all individuals, and in fact, is specifically *contraindicated* far more often than not.

This is also the case for other very specific types of therapies. There are specific indications for these, and you need and deserve expert help in referring you to the resources which you need. It is too confusing, haphazard, and potentially dangerous if you do not have help and guidance through this maze.

However, there are some overriding principles that might be helpful. I've often thought of all psychotherapy as a growth experience: we should be better as a result of it, not in spite of it! It is important that you trust your therapist, because you are turning over the very secrets of your inner being; your therapist must be worthy of that special trust. I also urge you to remember that therapy is for *your* emotional benefit—the benefit to the therapist is in the fee! If you have questions about this, discuss them openly with your therapist. It is the therapist's responsibility to ensure that you are not exploited by the therapeutic relationship.

Confidentiality is a critical factor in any therapeutic relationship. It *must* be a condition of the treatment contract, and you have a right to expect that the therapist will resist any outside efforts to invade this private relationship. When there are potential legal exceptions to this understanding, they should be discussed with you in full. You have a right to know the ground rules!

Now, let's move on to the individual types of psychotherapy.

As I mentioned before, "analysis" is a term that is used quite freely in the nonprofessional community. It is used to describe a wide range of "talk therapies." Actually, appropriate use of the term is quite narrow, limited, and specific. It refers to the psychoanalytical model, in which the goal is for the most complete evaluation and resolution of the patient's basic personality structure with its accompanying conflicts and adaptations. Psychoanalysis represents the "couch therapy'' that you have heard about, in which the therapist's role may seem quite passive. Actually, the psychoanalyst facilitates a regression and the emergence of unconscious thoughts by permitting silence and time lapses. Sigmund Freud, the author of the original studies about psychoanalysis, is universally accepted as the father of the technique.

It was from Freud's extensive work in developing psychoanalytical theory that we began to focus on such concepts as ''ego,'' ''superego,'' and ''id,'' as well as a system for describing consciousness—the preconscious, the unconscious—and psychosexual development. These principles of psychoanalysis are used extensively in psychoanalytical psychotherapy.

Freud was actually a physician trained in medicine and neurology, but his greatest legacy has been the psychoanalytic principles that he developed—an enormous undertaking.

Today, it is almost as if we have gone full circle. I mentioned before that psychiatrists and neurologists are now finding common areas of interest in current research. Whereas Dr. Freud started his professional career as a neurologist, then went on to devote his efforts to psychoanalysis, we are now witnessing a return to closer relationships between psychiatrists and neurologists once again.

In psychoanalysis, the technique focuses on the relationship between the analyst and the patient.

Psychodynamic psychotherapy, however, is designed to reduce symptoms by undertaking a less profound change in the personality. This is usually not done ''on the couch,'' but in face-to-face encounter with a more active therapist, with the focus of the therapy on the patient's life situation. This type of psychotherapy is primarily indicated in neurotic conflicts. It is not indicated in acute psychotic regression; however, it may be quite appropriate for someone who has been acutely psychotic, but is now relatively well compensated, if he has demonstrated the ability to respond to this type of long-term therapy.

Supportive psychotherapy represents a frequently utilized form of therapy—actually, I believe, utilized far more often than is acknowledged. This type of therapy does not attack the patient's defenses but rather focuses on helping the patient manage and control uncomfortable feelings and thoughts. This is done with reassurance and persuasion as well as suggestion. The focus is on current conflicts rather than exploration of the past or the unconscious.

Group Psychotherapy

Groups typically involve a therapist/leader and six to eight patients. Although initially viewed as a means of expanding therapeutic resources by treating several patients at one time, group therapy has become a valuable specific treatment modality that offers unique advantages. Careful selection of patients is important as the makeup of a particular group is considered; it can be done only after a thorough diagnostic assessment. There are many considerations in making the decision to use group therapy—a decision the therapist and patient should make together. These considerations include the diagnostic assessment of the patient, assessment of the patient's potential in therapy, and the patient's wishes. At times no other treatment form may be available.

Family therapy represents a type of group therapy; it is frequently recommended when there are signs of struggle within the family. Hopefully, the entire family will be available for the course of treatment. It is not unusual that members of a family are intent on maintaining the current situation and are resistant to change. This represents one of the early challenges of family therapy.

Behavioral and Cognitive Therapy

Behavioral therapy, contrary to the insight therapies we've been talking about, does not depend on an understanding of the unconscious, emotions, or feelings. Instead, it focuses on changing or removing signs and symptoms of disturbance. The theories behind behavioral therapy have given rise to several interesting techniques including desensitization, assertiveness training, sex therapy, and biofeedback. Behavioral therapy may be helpful for a patient with a repeated well-defined symptom—such as fear, compulsion, or obsession—that occurs in response to a specific outside stimulus.

A competent behavioral therapist will examine you carefully, evaluate all your signs and symptoms, and then make detailed recommendations on how to modify your daily routine or your approach to certain situations. The therapist should be prepared to explain any new terms, and to help you understand the reasons behind the treatment recommendations.

Cognitive therapy, a variation of the traditional behavioral approach, says that your response to a certain stimulus depends not on the stimulus itself, but on your interpretation (your "cognitive appraisal") of it. One woman responds to a red dress with sheer delight, while another thinks it's in very poor taste. A man who learned athletic skills in childhood feels confident about participating in sports as an adult, whereas a child with no exposure to athletics becomes a non-sports-oriented adult. These reactions—to the red dress or to sports opportunities—are learned responses, subject to the same laws as other kinds of behavior. Rewards and punishments, which are called positive and negative reinforcements, are the forces that form behavior.

Here's an example of how cognition can vary. Suppose several students stand up and walk out of a lecture. One teacher's response is, "What a shame; those kids who need to leave the room are going to miss the best part of my talk." A different teacher, whose self-esteem is low, begins to sweat and stammer, thinking to herself, "Those kids must be bored with my lecture. Darn it, I knew I should have spent more time preparing."

Cognitive behaviorists' term for the second teacher's destructive thoughts is "maladaptive behavior." They will use role-playing exercises and other techniques to help her replace her maladaptive responses with realistic and positive ones.

Behavioral and cognitive therapies are often successful in treating phobia, depression, and insomnia, and have some use in the treatment of problems like overeating, smoking, and hypertension. You should be aware, however, that when

Obstacles to Treatment:
Guilt, Denial, Codependency, and
Enabling

Alcoholism, depression, panic, anxiety, and other psychiatric conditions can strike without warning. Mistakenly attributing them to a lack of willpower only postpones seeking help. We now know that mental and emotional afflictions are not divine punishment for misdeeds, and that blaming the victim—or the victim's parents!—is a misapplication of psychoanalytic theory. Still, there are several common obstacles to seeking treatment:

I. Guilt, which of course helps no one, is often the greatest obstacle. A wife may feel guilty about her husband's uncontrollable rages. A husband may feel guilty about his wife's panicky fear of leaving the house. Parents of a drug abuser may feel guilty about "allowing" the problem to develop, or guilty about bringing the child for treatment. Children of a depressed mother may guiltily fear that their own behavior caused her depression.

II. Denial shrouds many psychiatric disorders. People with a drinking or drug problem, major depression, or a phobia may be afraid to acknowledge that they need help. Those with manic-depressive illness or a psychosis may be unaware that they even have a problem. Denial can extend to relatives, too: when a child has a learning disability, his parents may refuse to acknowledge it, angrily spurning the school's offer of special help.

III. Codependency and enabling are types of behavior seen not in psychiatric patients, but in their family members and friends.

If your child broke a leg, you'd rush to a doctor to

get the bone set. But what if the problem were mental or emotional? Perhaps your daughter is terrified of school, and you mistakenly think you're to blame. Perhaps your husband is an alcoholic, and you believe him when he says you drive him to drink. Perhaps your wife's severe mood swings baffle and upset you, and you think you can make her happy if you try just a little harder. In one of these situations, will you eagerly seek professional help? Possibly not.

In trying to maintain your own mental balance, you may choose to minimize the ill person's problem, make excuses for it, "live around" it. You may become this person's primary caretaker, rescuer, or excuse-maker. In the process, your own thoughts and reactions get warped. You no longer have a sure sense of what normal behavior is. At this point, you're said to be codependent. You enable the ill person to stay ill.

The codependent wife of an alcoholic, for example, may have grown up in a home where an alcoholic parent or sibling got all the attention. She developed a habit of measuring her self-worth by how much she could sacrifice to the alcoholic. Thus, when she grew up, she unwittingly chose as a marriage partner a "needy" alcoholic man whose dependency made her feel wanted.

A well-rounded psychiatric treatment program should treat not only the ill person, but his family members as well. Codependency is a habitual system of self-defeating thinking, feeling, and behaving. But with expert help, it's possible to abandon old, self-destructive habits and develop new, helpful ones.

used alone these therapies take no account of possible biological causes of psychiatric disorders. Psychiatrists may treat their patients with medication as well as with behavioral or cognitive therapy, thus addressing both the "physical" and the "mental" aspects of a disorder.

Other Approaches: The Humanist and Existentialist

There is at least one area in which psychodynamic and behavioral psychotherapists agree: In their efforts to identify cause-and-effect relationships, these therapists isolate behavior into separate components. Like the botanist who can follow the chain of discrete chemical reactions in the production of a dandelion, both behavioral and psychodynamic practitioners try to reduce a disorder such as depression to specific causes.

Humanists and existentialist therapists directly oppose this approach, asserting that to study human nature along the lines of natural science disregards the vital aspect of subjectivity. They contend that human learning is not naturalistic; it is experienced as a unity, a whole, not a sequence of separate components. They argue that living is complex and occurs in context, not as isolated phenomena. For these therapists, human learning takes place over time and cannot be frozen into a formula of past causes and present results.

For the humanist and the existentialist, the primary factor is human consciousness: our unique ability to be keenly aware of ourselves. This keen awareness dramatically affects and complicates our behavior. For the humanist and the existentialist, this separates human beings from other forms of life and is crucial to psychotherapy.

The humanist and existential approaches may help some individuals struggling with less severe psychiatric problems: the death of a loved one, dissatisfaction with one's career or personal relationships, or adjusting to a divorce. However, like other forms of psychotherapy, the humanistic and existential therapies fail to address the biological aspects of many common psychiatric disorders. A biologically depressed patient of one of these therapists may learn to understand the world better, but will still suffer from depression unless the biochemical imbalance is addressed when such an imbalance is the cause of the depression.

In this chapter, we have discussed some of the more common therapies a patient may encounter when first opening the treatment door. The choices and diversity can be quite intimidating. However, I strongly urge that each patient question prospective therapists thoroughly. It is not easy to ask these questions; nevertheless, it is your health and well-being that are at risk.

Some questions you may want to ask are:

1. Have you treated many patients with this problem before?
2. How long should treatment last?
3. Can my condition result from a physical disorder? If so, are you capable of diagnosing and treating this condition?
4. What do you think should be the goal of treatment?
5. How will we measure progress toward meeting this goal?
6. Would you help me arrange for a second opinion if I request this?
7. What are the alternatives available to me?

If the therapist has difficulty answering these questions, or if you are not confident in his or her ability to treat your problem, you should consider seeking another therapist.

In the next chapter, I'll discuss some of the various pitfalls that may prevent you from seeking treatment or from complying with a treatment plan.

Good luck!

2

CHILDREN, TEENAGERS, AND THE ELDERLY

Psychiatric disorders know no age limits. Children, teenagers, and the elderly are just as vulnerable to these problems as adults in the prime of life. All troubled individuals—and their families—can benefit from expert evaluation and proper treatment.

Psychiatric disorders always place a burden on the family, but when these problems occur in a child, adolescent, or an aging parent, the strain can be much greater. A surprising number of families have experienced this strain. Consider these statistics:

- As many as 1 in 5 children may have a psychiatric disorder serious enough to interfere with their lives. Unfortunately, 80 percent of these children *never* receive psychiatric care for their problems.
- Over 50,000 children are in mental health facilities.
- People over the age of 65 account for 25 percent of all suicides, even though they constitute only 12 percent of the general population.

Hopefully the enlightened adult and parent realizes that many psychiatric disorders may have a biological basis, and that the majority of these problems can be treated successfully. Unfortunately, though, far too many parents neglect to seek psychiatric treatment for their children or to encourage their elderly parents to seek help. They may mistakenly believe that the actions of their loved ones are a normal "phase" in development. Often their beliefs stem from ignorance concerning which signs and symptoms may indicate a psychiatric disorder.

This chapter briefly discusses the more common disorders among children, adolescents, and the elderly, while presenting some common warning signs for these disorders. Recognizing these signs is important, but can be very difficult. Many of these disorders overlap: a drug-abusing teenager may also be suffering from depression; an eating disorder victim may also have an anxiety disorder. Correctly "diagnosing" a family member's psychiatric difficulty may lie outside the grasp of even the most astute layperson. Therefore, if you have *any* concerns regarding the mental health of a family member, a mental health professional should be consulted. (In addition to the following passages, more detailed information regarding specific conditions and their treatment may be found in Section II.)

Psychiatric Disorders of Children and Adolescents

The most common psychiatric disorders of childhood and adolescence are:

1. Attention-deficit hyperactivity disorder
2. Conduct disorders
3. Substance abuse
4. Eating disorders

Both attention-deficit hyperactivity disorder (ADHD) and conduct disorder (CD) have been classified as *disruptive disorders*.

Disruptive disorders should not be confused with exaggerated cases of the "terrible twos," prolonged childhood, immaturity, or emotional repression; in some cases, disruptive disorders arise from biological problems, although the exact nature of the biological problem is not fully understood.

The disruptive child is unable to insert judgment between impulse and action. He seems to spread disaster in his wake. Parents and teachers believe the child does it on purpose. Peers think he is a troublemaker.

These children usually suffer from low self-esteem, seeing themselves as inadequate. They feel misunderstood and tend to blame others for their problems. In fact, an important aspect of psychiatric treatment is to help the child develop a sense of responsibility. These youngsters can lead normal, happy lives if psychiatric treatment is sought early. The two most common disruptive disorders are ADHD and CD. These disorders are profiled in Section II.

Drugs: A Trap for Teens

As we're all aware from reading the papers and watching the news, drug abuse is a major problem in the United States. Part of the trouble is the sheer availability of drugs of all kinds.

Alcohol, this nation's favorite mood-altering drug, is theoretically harder for teens to get now that many states have raised the drinking age. But most kids find ways around these restrictions, including drinking from their own family's liquor cabinet. Others have no trouble getting older friends to buy beer for them.

Potent and illegal mood-altering drugs such as **cocaine** and **crack** (a smokable form of cocaine) are cheaper and more easily available than ever before. Both of these drugs cause manic, "hyper" behavior, and are responsible for an increased incidence of homicide and other violent crime.

Marijuana, popular in the 1960s, is now prevalent in far more powerful forms.

LSD and other hallucinogenic drugs dropped out of favor during the 1970s, but made a comeback in the late 1980s.

PCP (phencyclidine, "angel dust"), a cheap and very dangerous illegal drug, gives a sensation of elation and power but can also cause paranoia, disturbed vision, and mental breakdown.

Various prescription medications, especially **tranquilizers**, lend themselves to abuse by teens, who take the pills from the family medicine cabinet.

The Signs of Drug Abuse

Unfortunately, it's all too easy to overlook the signs of drug abuse in your own teenager. First, your child may be very clever at concealing the evidence. Second, you may not know what to look for. And third, you probably have a natural tendency to blame your teen's objectionable behavior on simple rebelliousness, not drug use.

But it's a mistake to look the other way. Teenagers who abuse alcohol and drugs are a danger to others and to themselves. They are likely to be involved in auto accidents. They may easily slide into promiscuity or criminal behavior in an effort to support their drug use. They are at a great risk for suicide. Friends, hobbies, schoolwork, sports—everything important in their lives—may go down the drain if they get caught in the insidious spiral of drug dependency. Plus many young people whose drug-dependent behavior continues unchecked get stuck at a halfway point in the maturing process. Instead of growing up and assuming adult responsibilities—college, trade school, a job—they may become aimless, luckless drifters.

Thus, if you're the parent of an adolescent child, it pays to be aware of the early warning signs of a possible alcohol- or drug-dependency problem. There may be cause for concern if you notice any of the following:

- **Two or more clear instances of drug abuse**, whether the child was drunk, stoned, or otherwise high.

- **A suicide attempt** involving an overdose of a medication or drug.
- **Regular use** of alcohol and drugs even after you've taken a firm stand against it.
- **Academic trouble** for a child who was formerly a good student.
- **Family turmoil** caused when the teenager picks fights incessantly or refuses to do regular chores.
- **Personality changes** for the worse.
- **Rundown state of health**, perhaps including frequent sore throats, coughing, red eyes, a pasty look, or a dull, listless attitude.
- **Drug-culture clothes**, such as T-shirts with insignia of heavy-metal rock groups.
- **Legal trouble**—anything from stealing and shoplifting through vandalism and traffic arrests.
- **Undesirable new friends** unlike the kids your teenager hung out with before.
- **A sudden mysterious supply of money** that obviously isn't from an allowance or a job. Kids who deal drugs often have a lot of money.

If you do suspect your adolescent has even a mild alcohol or drug dependency, it's very important that you seek out a psychiatric service that specializes in evaluating teens with this type of problem. Remember, you yourself don't have to decide if your youngster has a problem. That's a job for experienced professionals who are trained to interview the individual and decide if blood and urine tests should be done before reaching a conclusion. All you need to do is set up the appointment and make sure your son or daughter gets there on time. If the evaluation does indicate a probable alcohol of drug problem, you and your child will have various treatment options to choose from. And if the evaluation uncovers not drug dependency, but another type of problem, then you'll be in a better position to seek help for what's really wrong.

Eating Disorders

Anorexia nervosa is an eating disorder that ends fatally in 5 to 18 percent of cases. It is far more prevalent among girls and young women today than it was a few decades ago. Contrary to what you might suppose, the anorectic—who survives on almost no food, stays at least 15 percent below the lower limit for normal body weight, and puts herself at risk for death by starvation or cardiac arrest—does not lose her appetite. Instead, she exercises furiously to burn calories and meanwhile maintains a firm control over what she eats. She tries very hard to achieve a goal of thinness even when, by objective standards, she has long since reached that goal.

Part of the disorder is a distorted body image. The young woman may be alarmingly thin and yet persists in feeling she is "too fat." When menstruation stops, as it usually does in anorexia, she may be pleased that she has achieved freedom from this function of female sexuality. No amount of coaxing, urging, or threatening from family or friends can induce her to relax her vigilance and begin eating enough to gain back the lost weight. When she is profoundly underweight, her body temperature, heartbeat, and blood pressure may drop below normal, and she may develop a growth of fine body hair (lanugo hair) similar to that seen on newborn babies. She is likely to deny that she is ill, and to resist therapy.

Bulimia, another common eating disorder, involves a binge-and-purge pattern. Typically, the bulimic person is a young woman who, dissatisfied with her weight, tries to maintain a diet, but then gives in—usually secretly—to an overwhelming desire to eat. When she's sure no one will see her, the bulimic wolfs down huge quantities of food, preferably sugary or starchy food, to satisfy her craving. During the binge, her urge to eat seems beyond her control. Once sated, she loathes herself for "pigging out." She follows the binge with a purge, using self-induced vomiting, laxatives, diuretics, or all three to cleanse her body of the excess load of food.

Unlike the anorectic, the bulimic young woman avoids a state of near-starvation. As she continues to binge and purge, her weight fluctuates between a high point and a low point. Psychologically, she suffers from an obsessive concern about her weight and about when, what, and how much to eat; she feels that conflicts about eating dominate her life. Physically, she suffers from the effects of constant purging: strong stomach acid from repeated vomiting may erode the enamel on her teeth; chronic laxative use may give her a "lazy bowel" and chronic constipation; excessive diuretic use may upset her body's electrolyte balance, exposing her to dehydration, heart arrhythmias, and even sudden death.

It's possible for a person to have a combination of anorexia and bulimia.

Since eating disorders are potentially very serious problems, it's well to be aware of their signs and symptoms and to seek treatment for your child right away if you suspect she has one of these conditions (see section II for the symptoms of eating disorders). Although this advice may sound obvious, several things may conspire against early recognition of an eating disorder:

- A stressful situation sometimes may appear to precipitate anorexia nervosa. If the stressful event is something that touches the entire family, such as a move to a new town or the death of a relative, everyone may be temporarily too preoccupied to notice the beginnings of an adolescent's anorexia. The result is a failure to recognize the development of this very serious illness until it is in a late stage of development.
- Many girls who become anorexic are known as perfectionists in everything they undertake. If a determined, perfectionist girl who is slightly overweight sets out to lose weight and seems to be succeeding, everyone may simply assume this is just one more example of her admirable willpower. These patients frequently seem to be in charge and in control of themselves. In reality, her behavior is another example of the disorder. By missing this sign, the family fails to detect an early sign of a developing eating disorder.

It may be a while before her family realizes that the weight-loss effort has spun out of control.
• Anorexia and bulimia tend to run in families. This may mean there's a biological predisposition involved, or it may mean that children learn attitudes about food from their parents. An overweight mother might deflect her dissatisfaction with her own body by criticizing her daughter's weight, thus unintentionally encouraging an obsession in the daughter about food and eating. In addition, a mother who is preoccupied with her own binge-and-purge cycle may not recognize the development of the same pattern in her daughter.

Suicide: Teen Tragedy

Young people aged 15 to 25 years are the only age group in this country with a steadily rising mortality rate; suicide among this group is the fastest-growing cause of death. Almost 500,000 teenagers attempt suicide each year, and nearly 5,000 are successful. This is a national tragedy when you acknowledge that these young people are our greatest resource and represent our future.

Severe depression frequently represents the underlying illness. Suicide is the most severe symptom—thus depression is a potentially fatal disease. Most people think of depression as something that happens only to grownups, but psychiatrists are increasingly aware that teenagers and even children can suffer from full-scale clinical depression. Interestingly, a depressed youngster may not seem sad, despondent, or morose at all. Instead, he may seem primarily sullen and irritable, showing periodic bursts of anger. It's important for parents to know that irritability in a child may be a sign of depression, rather than evidence of "spoiling" or simple bad temper.

Delinquent teenagers—those who have what's known as conduct disorder (repeated, intentional violation of other people's personal and property rights)—are more likely than other young people to turn their angry impulses against themselves in suicide attempts. If a delinquent youngster is depressed, the risk of suicide is even greater.

Teens with alcohol and drug problems are also at risk for suicide. Despair over an uncontrollable drug dependency may precipitate suicide, or the suicide may be an "unintentional" result of drug overdosage. In some cases, drug abuse causes temporary psychosis: a young person so high that he is "out of his head" may be convinced he can fly, and may decide to test this new ability—with predictable results. Finally, a person's judgment may be significantly impaired while intoxicated, contributing to dangerous, reckless, and potentially fatal behavior.

Depression, delinquency, drug dependency: since any one of these conditions may increase a youngster's risk for suicide, all three are warning signs to parents of adolescents. If one of them describes your youngster, it's time to get serious about looking for professional help.

We talked about denial in Chapter 1. Denial of obvious signs and symptoms frequently interferes with early recognition and initiation of appropriate treatment. Such is the case when parents fail or refuse to recognize the early signs of ADHD, conduct disorder, drug abuse, eating disorders, and depression. Take time to stop and carefully look for denial. It's not only tricky, but risky.

The "Golden Age"

The American population is getting older. In 1984, the American Association of Retired Persons reported 28 million Americans over the age of 65. With reduced population growth and increased life expectancy, there are proportionally fewer young people and more elderly people than at any time in our country's history. This trend is expected to continue.

As the "graying of America" progresses, we seem to be getting over some of our former national obsession with youth. Of course, plenty of people still dread the approach of their

40th birthday, the gateway to middle age. But senior citizens—those aged 65 and older—are gaining in public stature, media visibility, and political clout. This country is paying more attention to the older generation than ever before.

Trends in mental health care reflect these developments, with geriatric psychiatry one of the fastest-growing sectors in the field. If you're one of the millions of American adults taking care of a parent or a parent-in-law, you already have some insight into the medical, social, and emotional issues that touch an older person's life.

The aging person has to cope with a certain amount of inevitable physical decline: failing eyesight or hearing, joints stiff or painful from arthritis, reduced strength and stamina. Medications given to treat various illnesses may have particularly strong side effects in an older person, since the aging kidney and other organs have a reduced capacity to wash drug residues out of the body.

After retirement or the death of a spouse, the older person may face a big adjustment to a different mode of life: loss of a job that had provided structure, meaning, and social interaction; a sharply curtailed annual income and thus a reduced standard of living; a move to a smaller house or to an apartment, perhaps without a yard or garden, perhaps far from the old familiar neighborhood.

As more and more friends and relatives die, the older person is forced to modify his perspective on life. He may philosophically accept the continuing chain of losses, acknowledging that death is indeed a part of life. Or he may fear and resent these unrelenting losses, and sink into a more or less permanent mood of pessimism.

Depression in Older People

We mentioned before that depression in a young person can masquerade as anger and irritability. In the elderly, the problem is slightly different. Depression may look exactly the way we might expect—sadness, tearfulness, inattention to basic grooming, lack of interest in life—but we may assume, *mistakenly*, that this is an inevitable part of growing old.

In fact, depression in the elderly is often just as amenable to psychiatric treatment as depression in a younger person. The key to treatment is discovering the cause. For this reason, it's important to evaluate all the possible physical factors.

The elderly consume a full 25 percent of all prescribed medications. Older patients who have several chronic conditions—for example, heart trouble, high blood pressure, ulcers, arthritis, or diabetes—are apt to be taking numerous medications, any one of which may cause depression as a side effect. Furthermore, the more different kinds of medication a person takes, the greater the chance that these medications will interact with each other in unpredictable ways. One possible effect is depression.

Sometimes a change of medication is all it takes to clear up an older person's long-standing depression. Certain blood-pressure medications have been linked with depression; an alternative medication may provide the same blood-pressure control without the emotional side effect.

On the other hand, depressed mood in an elderly patient may actually stem from *lack* of treatment of a medical condition. When she receives adequate treatment for her arthritis, that sunny disposition may reemerge.

Some older people really do suffer from classic major depression, and may be helped by antidepressant medication. It's especially important to get competent psychiatric help, since the elderly often react to antidepressants differently from young people. Tricyclic antidepressants, usually the medications of choice for younger patients, may not be suitable for older individuals, especially those who have heart conditions. Sometimes it's feasible to give the older depressed patient a monoamine oxidase inhibitor (MAOI), an entirely different type of antidepressant medication that requires the patient to stick to a special diet. If the danger of drug interactions makes it inadvisable to treat with any form of antidepressant medication, electroshock therapy may offer considerable relief to the depressed older patient. It may be a safer course of treatment in a patient of this age group.

Suicide is a frequent complication of depression in this age group. The rate of suicide is highest among the elderly. A very real public health hazard, suicide is preventable—but we must recognize and react if we are to have an opportunity at prevention.

Confusion and Dementia

If your aging parent becomes vague and confused, do not jump to the immediate conclusion that he is getting senile. Confusion and senility do occur in some older people, of course, but there are various other possible explanations, all of which deserve consideration. A psychiatrist can help sort through the possible causes of mental confusion.

As we've seen, interactions between two or more medications commonly occur in older people. One patient may react by becoming depressed. Another may react with confusion and disorientation. To get rid of this confusion it may be necessary to switch one or more of the medications, or perhaps eliminate a medication altogether. Naturally, these medication adjustments need to be made carefully and professionally. A psychiatrist often needs to consult with the elderly patient's other doctors to determine what adjustments are possible and desirable.

Self-medication can cause considerable problems. When Martha, aged 78, complained of insomnia, her regular doctor gave her a prescription for sleeping pills. Martha liked the effect of the pills, and began taking them during the day, too, hoping to drop off for a little nap when she was bored. Unfortunately, the pills made her dizzy and groggy. She began having trouble speaking clearly and walking steadily. Her daughter, with whom she lived, was very concerned that her mother was rapidly losing both her mental clarity and her sense of balance. Then one day she happened to see Martha downing a sleeping pill in midafternoon, and she put two and two together. Sure enough, as soon as she made sure the sleeping pills were out of sight, except at bedtime, her mother's alertness and coordination returned as if by magic.

Few older people are interested in illegal drugs, but some may be alcohol abusers. One 94-year-old woman was mistakenly diagnosed as having Alzheimer's disease. Then an alert psychiatrist discovered that she was combining over-the-counter sleeping medication with nearly a pint of whisky a day—a habit she had fallen into after her husband died several years previously. This doctor persuaded his patient to stop drinking, and he prescribed a more effective sleeping medication. When she followed this treatment plan, her "Alzheimer's" symptoms abated remarkably.

Coping With the Caretaker Role

Finally, you may need to evaluate what your own life has become if you are the primary caretaker for your aging parent(s) or in-law(s). Many people in their 40s and 50s—some still raising their own children—suddenly find themselves becoming "parents to their parents" when illness or infirmity strikes their mother or father. Perhaps you welcome an aging parent into your home without question or hesitation. Suddenly you find yourself in the role of caretaker or, if you still have children at home, double-caretaker. This can be a source of both tremendous personal satisfaction and considerable physical and emotional strain.

If you find that you're overcome with caretaking worries, you may need to seek psychiatric guidance for yourself. There may be approaches to your responsibilities—nursing home, senior citizen housing, home health aide, adult day care program, meals on wheels—that you've never seriously considered before. A professional who's emotionally removed from your family situation is in an excellent position to help you see your options more clearly. It's worth your while to seek professional, impartial help in figuring out how best to "do right by" your parents, your children, your spouse, and yourself—all at the same time!

3

PSYCHIATRIC MEDICATIONS

Imagine a time when a physician would describe life in a typical mental institution with these words:

> Catatonic patients stood day after day, rigid as statues, their legs swollen and bursting with dependent edema [swelling]. Their comrades idled week after week, lying on hard benches or the floor, aware only of their delusions and hallucinations. Others were . . . pacing back and forth like caged animals in a zoo. Periodically, the air was pierced by the shouts of a raving maniac. Suddenly, without notice, like an erupting volcano, an anergic schizophrenic bursts into frenetic behavior, lashing out at others or striking himself with his fists, or running wildly and aimlessly about.
>
> Nurses and attendants, ever in danger, spent their time protecting patients from harming themselves or others . . . For lack of more effective remedies, they secluded dangerously frenetic individuals behind thick doors in barred rooms stripped of all furniture and lacking toilet facilities. They restrained many others in cuffs and jack-

ets or chained them to the floors and walls. Daily they
sent patients for hydrotherapy, where they were im-
mersed for long hours in tubs or were packed in wet
sheets . . . (Ayd, F. J. and Blackwell, B. eds. *Discoveries in Biological Psychiatry,* Philadelphia: J. B. Lippincott, 1970.)

Was this physician describing the primitive psychiatry of
the nineteenth or even eighteenth century?

No, the physician actually described the typical psychiatric
hospital just *thirty-seven years ago*! At a time when the world
had already entered the atomic age, when penicillin, televi-
sion, and trans-Atlantic flights were changing life as it had
been known, psychiatry was still confined to these "dark age"
practices.

But the field of psychiatry would soon change. What happened to move psychiatry into the modern age?

In a word: *psychopharmacology.*

Briefly, psychopharmacology refers to the use of medications to treat psychiatric conditions. For centuries, men and
women have known the power of potions over the mind—
Homer, for instance, wrote of the power of the lotus leaf to
sedate.

But in the 1950s, through the hard work and good fortune
of researchers, psychiatry began to refine this basic knowledge into treatment tools. Over the past thirty years, I have
been fortunate enough to witness firsthand the development
of new medications and the enhancement of existing medications. Psychiatry now boasts a wide array of pharmacologic
tools to treat many psychiatric conditions. The psychiatric
practices of 1950 have been significantly complemented.
While it would be misleading to claim that psychopharmacology was solely responsible for these changes, nevertheless
it was—without question—among the dominant forces behind
the revolution. Millions of patients have benefited enor-
mously from its effects.

But along with the power and benefits of psychopharmacology come *responsibility*. Responsible patients:

1. Understand the need to take their medication properly
2. Comply with their physician's instructions
3. Report side effects promptly to their doctor

The backbone that supports a patient's responsibility is information.

Regrettably, some physicians neglect to inform their patients properly, or patients—in the anxiety that often accompanies a visit to the doctor—may not remember what they've been told. This lack of information can have several deleterious effects, from ignorance of potentially harmful side effects to the patient's failure to take the medication as directed.

To help both patient and physician to overcome this information gap, the following section lists important questions for patients to ask their doctor or pharmacist regarding medication. Patients can take these questions to the doctor's office, along with a pad and pencil to write down the answers.

Questions to Ask a Doctor

1. When should the medication be taken? The time at which you take the medication—before or after a meal, before going to bed, or when you first awaken—may affect the drug's ability to work, as well as minimize any potential side effects.

2. Are there any foods, drinks, or other medications to be avoided? Some people are surprised to learn that certain combinations of food, drinks, or medications can result either in the medication not working well, or in potentially harmful side effects. For example, a common class of antidepressants called MAO inhibitors should never be taken with foods or drinks containing *tyramine*, such as cheeses, wine, smoked meats, and other food substances.

3. Should any activities by avoided? Some medications can cause drowsiness and/or poor coordination; therefore, your doctor may suggest that you not drive a car or operate heavy machinery while taking the medication. Other medications may react with sunlight; therefore, your doctor may suggest that you restrict your exposure to sunlight.

4. What side effects may arise? This question is crucial. Some physicians may hesitate to discuss potential side effects, fearing that the information will frighten the patient unnecessarily. In reality, the patient should not be frightened, but appropriately concerned. Most side effects are minor and will usually pass quickly. In general, serious side effects to well-established medications are rare. Nevertheless, it is the duty of the physician to explain the warning signs of potential side effects, and of the patient to report these effects promptly.

5. If side effects do occur, should the medication be discontinued? In general, the administration of a medication should be discontinued only if the physician explicitly tells the patient to stop taking the medication when a particular side effect occurs. Otherwise, the patient should not cease taking the medication without the physician's knowledge. If any troublesome side effect does occur, the patient should always inform the doctor immediately.

6. How should medications be stored? Most medications should be stored in a cool, dark, and dry place, away from a child's reach. Childproof caps should always be used if children are present. Ask your physician if you should keep unused medications for future use.

In addition to the above questions, there are a few **rules** patients should never break:

Rule #1: Never use another person's prescription.
Rule #2: Never take more than the prescribed dose.
Rule #3: Take the prescription exactly as prescribed.
Rule #4: Always inform the physician of any other medications you may be taking, or of any past or current health problem.
Rule #5: Always tell the doctor if you are pregnant or planning to become pregnant.

In addition to following these rules and receiving helpful instructions from a physician, most patients benefit from a basic understanding of the major types of psychiatric medication. Hopefully, this information will help a patient to better understand why a particular medication was recommended, and why continued compliance with the treatment plan is so important. The following section addresses this basic level of knowledge. However, a patient with any questions or concerns regarding a particular medication should always consult the physician; there is no substitute for a good physician's experience and knowledge.

In general, antidepressant medications can be divided into three categories: the tricyclic antidepressants (and related compounds), the monoamine oxidase inhibitors (MAOIs), and a relatively new category of drugs that affect the neurotransmitter called *serotonin*. (Neurotransmitters are chemical messengers responsible for carrying information between nerve cells.)

Like other conditions in medicine, researchers have been unable to discover exactly what causes clinical depression (also called unipolar depression). While the process of regulating moods is extremely complex, many researchers believe that the neurotransmitters serotonin and norepinephrine play important roles in depression. Normally these neurotransmitters work to keep us from getting too euphoric (manic) or too depressed. Any biological deficiency or disruption in this regulatory system may result in depression, mania, or manic-depression (also called bipolar depression).

In general, antidepressants work by affecting levels of one or both of these neurotransmitters, thereby restoring our regulatory system. Usually, tricyclic antidepressants (TCAs) are the treatment of choice.

The first antidepressant, imipramine, was approved in 1957. Since that time a number of studies have shown TCAs to be extremely effective in relieving depression. Which tricyclic antidepressant should be tried first may depend upon a number of factors, such as a patient's response to specific diagnostic tests and potential side effects.

For the 10 to 30 percent who fail to respond to TCAs, or who cannot tolerate their side effects, the MAOIs may be tried. MAOIs, first discovered over thirty years ago, are thought to relieve depression by inhibiting the monoamine enzyme. Monoamine appears to break down certain neurotransmitters. By inhibiting these enzymes, the MAOIs treat

The Major Types of Medication

Antidepressant Medications

Generic Name	Brand Name(s)*
Amitriptyline	Elavil
	Endep
	Available as generic
Amoxapine	Asendin
Clomipramine	Anafranil
Desipramine	Norpramin
	Pertofrane
Doxepin	Adapin
	Sinequan
	Available as generic
Fluoxetine	Prozac
Imipramine	Janimine
	Tofranil
	Available as generic
Maprotiline	Ludiomil
Nortriptyline	Pamelor
Protriptyline	Vivactil
Trazodone	Desyrel
	Available as generic
Trimipramine	Surmontil
MAO Inhibitors:	
Isocarboxazid	Marplan
Phenelzine	Nardil
Tranylcypromine	Parnate

depression by affecting the levels of neurotransmitters in the brain.

The most serious factor limiting the use of MAOIs concerns their potential for serious side effects. As I discussed earlier in this chapter, the combination of MAOIs with foods

*The brand names listed in this section do not constitute a complete list, but merely reflect some of the more common brands.

containing tyramine may result in a serious, even fatal, hypertensive crisis. Therefore patients taking MAOIs must follow strict dietary rules. Foods to be avoided include: aged meats and cheese, beer, wine, chocolate, coffee, pickled herring, yeast, chicken liver, and nonpasteurized yogurt. In addition, certain medications, such as amphetamines and some over-the-counter allergy and cold preparations, should be avoided. Patients taking MAOIs should ask their physician for a complete list of dietary and drug restrictions.

In addition to their role as antidepressants, both the TCAs and MAOIs have been used to treat other psychiatric conditions. In fact, TCAs are the treatment of first choice for a very common anxiety disorder called Panic Disorder. Other conditions that may benefit from antidepressant therapy include eating disorders, obsessive-compulsive disorder, mood swings, and drug and alcohol withdrawal.

Antipsychotic Medications

Generic Name	Brand Name(s)
Acetophenazine maleate	Tindal
Chlorpromazine hydro-chloride	Thorazine
	Available as generic
Chlorprothixine	Taractan
Fluphenazine hydrochloride	Permitil
	Prolixin
	Available as generic
Haloperidol	Haldol
Mesoridazine besylate	Serentil
Molindone hydrochloride	Moban
Perphenazine	Trilafon
Pimozide	Orap
Prochlorperazine	Compazine
	Available as generic
Thioridazine hydrochloride	Mellaril
	Available as generic
Thiothixene	Navane
	Available as generic

Generic Name	Brand Name(s)
Trifluoperazine hydro-chloride	Stelazine
	Available as generic
Triflupromazine hydro-chloride	Vesprin

These medications, sometimes referred to as major tranquilizers, are also used to treat psychoses, such as schizophrenia.

While no one knows exactly how antipsychotics work, some experts believe that they work by affecting a neurotransmitter in the brain called dopamine. The specific neurotransmitter dopamine is thought to be involved with psychotic behavior. According to this theory, an excess of dopamine causes rapid chemical reactions within the brain—reactions that occur so quickly that the brain cannot handle the information overload. These rapid reactions result in psychotic behavior, including such symptoms as delusions and hallucinations.

Antipsychotic medications appear to work by reducing the excess levels of dopamine, which may enable chemical reactions within the brain to proceed at a more normal rate. These agents have allowed a significant number of otherwise psychotic individuals to lead normal lives at home and in the workplace.

These medications are powerful, however, and with that power comes the element of risk. Perhaps the most significant risk concerns the potential for a serious side effect called tardive dyskinesia. Tardive dyskinesia is characterized by sudden jerks of the head, neck, trunk, tongue, or body. Studies have found that this condition may occur in 10 to 20 percent of patients taking antipsychotic medications for a year or more. This side effect *may* disappear even without withdrawing or reducing the dosage. However, some patients must either have their dosage reduced or withdrawn completely. Regrettably, some patients continue to experience tardive dyskinesia even after they have stopped taking the medication.

For this reason, the American Psychiatric Association has

established these stringent guidelines to reduce the possibility of tardive dyskinesia:

1. Antipsychotic drugs should be reserved for the short-term treatment of acute psychosis, including first attacks or exacerbation of schizophrenia, paranoia, mania, some cases of toxic or organic brain psychoses, childhood psychoses, and as adjuncts to psychotic depression.

2. Long-term use (greater than six months) is recommended only for chronic psychotic disorders, especially schizophrenia, and only when the patient continues to respond to the medication.

3. Antipsychotic therapy should be evaluated once a year by reducing the dosage by 10 percent every three to seven days until either the medication has been stopped or the patient's condition worsens.

There are other potentially serious side effects including changes in the blood system and damage to the liver. It is for these reasons that the patient should be followed at regular intervals by a clinician who is experienced with these agents. It is important that there be an opportunity for the clinician to observe any side effects as soon as they appear, and to make needed adjustments to the dosage or the type of medication.

Clearly, both physician and patient should consider the risk of taking these medications versus the benefits to be gained from the antipsychotic medications.

Antianxiety Medications

Generic Name	Brand Name(s)
Benzodiazepines	
Alprazolam	Xanax
Chlordiazepoxide	Librium
Clonazepam	Klonopin
Clorazepate dipotassium	Tranxene
Diazepam	Valium

Generic Name	Brand Name(s)
Benzodiazepines	
Flurazepam*	Dalmane
Halazepam	Paxipam
Lorazepam*	Ativan
Oxazepam*	Serax
Prazepam*	Centrax
Temazepam*	Restoril
Triazolam	Halcion
Barbiturates	
Amobarbital	Amytal
Mephobarbital	Mebaral
Pentobarbital	Nembutal
Phenobarbital*	Solfoton
Secobarbital	Seconal sodium

available as generic

The benzodiazepines (and their derivatives) are the most widely prescribed medications in America. Their popularity primarily results from two factors: anxiety disorders—the most common psychiatric ailment (and for which benzodiazepines are indicated), and the fact that some physicians have overused these medications.

Without question, benzodiazepines provide effective short-term relief for many forms of anxiety. However, some physicians prescribe benzodiazepines needlessly, for anxiety and/or insomnia that are temporary and transient. Panic disorder patients—who do not usually respond to most benzodiazepines, with the exception of alprazolam—are often prescribed these medications incorrectly because their panic symptoms may resemble other anxiety disorders (such as generalized anxiety disorder) that do respond to benzodiazepines. In addition, some physicians prescribe these medications for too great a time period or at too high a dosage level, thereby greatly increasing their potential for abuse and addiction. Additionally, they are sometimes prescribed for symptoms of anxiety with which we are all familiar and which should be expected as part of our daily lives. The use of these drugs should be reserved for abnormal levels of anxiety and when the symptoms are pathologic and greater than that experienced by most other people.

In general, the overall effectiveness among the benzodiazepines is similar. Usually, the actual benzodiazepine chosen depends upon the physician's experience and the potential for side effects. The shorter-acting benzodiazepines, such as alprazolam, lorazepam, and oxazepam, may benefit individuals who must stay very alert. However, the shorter-acting drugs may require more frequent (and inconvenient) dosing, especially if anxiety reappears between doses.

Mood Stabilizers

Carbamezapine	Tegretol
Clonazepam	Klonopin
Lithium	Depakote
Valproic Acid	

Manic-depressive disorder (also called bipolar disorder) is the most serious form of mood swings. A manic-depressive patient experiences episodes of incredible euphoria (mania) followed by periods of deep depression. Other less severe forms of mood swings include patients diagnosed as rapid cyclers (cyclothymics), hypomanics, or bipolar II. In general, the treatment of choice for most mood swings is lithium.

Lithium's discovery resulted from almost equal parts of luck and intelligence. Some forty years ago the researcher John F. Cade attempted to find substances that might cause mental illness by injecting the urine of mental patients into guinea pigs. Cade then injected lithium carbonate simply to help the guinea pigs absorb the urine of the mental patients. Cade noticed that his pigs became very lethargic after the lithium injection. Remarkably, Cade then concluded that lithium might be useful in treating mental illness. Twenty years later, lithium was approved by the Food and Drug Administration for the treatment of bipolar disorder.

Until lithium use, manic-depressive patients had little choice but to depend on available antipsychotic agents for the periods of mania and available antidepressants for those alternating periods of depression. The result was sometimes a roller coaster ride of ups and downs with the aggressive medication sometimes contributing to the mood swings. Lithium changed much of that, and the lives of manic-depressives have improved immeasurably with its success.

Regrettably, approximately 20 percent of patients either cannot tolerate lithium's side effects or do not benefit from the drug.For those patients who fail to respond to lithium, other mood-stabilizing medications may be tried, either in combination with lithium or by themselves. Recently, many psychiatrists have turned to the anticonvulsant medication carbamazepine (Tegretol) to augment lithium therapy. In one study, 50 percent of patients who had failed to respond to lithium alone improved significantly when carbamazepine was tried. This drug appears to have a more positive effect on mania rather than depression, though antidepressant properties have been shown. Other medications that may be tried include the benzodiazepine drug clonazepam (Klonopin) and valproic acid (Depakene).

Psychostimulant Medication and Children

Dextroamphetamine sulfate	Dexedrine
	Available as generic
Pemoline	Cylert
Methylphenidate	Ritalin

No parents relish the thought of their child taking psychiatric medication. Over the years, I've encountered some parents who initially were adamant in their objection to medication, even when it was clearly the best course of treatment. While these parental objections are understandable, they interfere with the child receiving needed help.

When talking to parents about medication for their child, I often use a diabetes analogy: No parents welcome the thought of their child being injected with insulin, yet for the diabetic child the insulin injection is the difference between life and death. No responsible parents would deny their child the injection necessary to sustain life.

While not as life-threatening as diabetes, the disruptive disorders of childhood, such as attention-deficit hyperactivity disorder (ADHD), conduct disorder, and other behavioral disorders, if left untreated, can seriously interfere with normal function at home and in school and thus wreck a family's unity. Psychostimulant medications, such as methylphenidate (Ritalin), magnesium pemoline (Cylert), and dextroamphetamine sulfate (Dexedrine) have been used to treat an estimated 800,000 children suffering from ADHD and other behavioral disorders.

Recently, some groups have protested the use of psychiatric medications in children, claiming that these medications are used solely to control the child. In reality, numerous studies and the vast majority of child psychiatrists have found that medications are the most effective means of treating ADHD. When properly prescribed, these medications do not "control" the child; rather, they allow the child the ability to control himself.

Undoubtedly, psychostimulant medications have occasionally been administered improperly by physicians not trained in child psychiatry. To be used most effectively, psychostimulants should be used as part of a broad-based treatment approach, incorporating psychotherapy for the child and family therapy when necessary. Psychostimulant medications can actually facilitate the other forms of therapy by helping the child maintain attention span and gain control over impulses. This last point bears repeating: psychiatric medications, prescribed correctly, do not control the child; rather, they *allow the child to control himself*.

Often the greatest problem a child faces with taking a psychoactive medication is a social one. Most children shy away from anything that makes them stand out from others. Hopefully, the psychiatrist, parents, and school can all work together to make the process of pill-taking as unobtrusive as possible. If necessary, and whenever possible, longer-acting, slow-release forms of the medication may be used to prevent administration during school hours.

Parents play an important role in prescribing medication to children. The parents supervise the child and see that medication is taken properly, at the right time and at the right dosage. Parents must ask the physician the same questions listed above and must report quickly to the psychiatrist any changes or side effects of the medication, since children can not be relied upon to report these changes accurately.

4

INPATIENTS, OUTPATIENTS, AND THE DIFFERENT TYPES OF TREATMENT

Most individuals have some idea—even if it's a mistaken one—of how a counseling session in a psychiatrist's or therapist's private office might proceed. And most people have heard of—or at least read about—a psychiatric hospital. But many people are not aware of any treatment between these two extremes.

In fact, there is a continuum of available treatment resources, and several treatment alternatives may be planned for a given patient. You'll have a much easier time finding the type of treatment that's right for you or your loved one if you know the range of available options. In this chapter we'll take a look at the spectrum of possible treatment alternatives, starting with the most restrictive setting and proceeding to the least restrictive. Good treatment plans will utilize the least restrictive setting which is suitable for the problem. (Please note that the following classifications are general.)

Inpatient Care

Let's assume, for example, that in searching your geographic area for possible treatment centers you discover a facility that calls itself "Milestone Manor." The name itself gives you little information. Is this a residential treatment facility for troubled teenagers? A halfway house for schizophrenic adults? A three-quarter house for recovering alcoholics? You'll need to make a phone call to learn more.

Psychiatric patients are admitted to inpatient care settings because of the symptoms they present—not because of the diagnosis. As an example, a depressive diagnosis does not dictate the use of the hospital; however, depression complicated by serious suicidal behavior does require hospitalization.

The following questions may be used to help you determine the type of treatment facility that lies behind the name.

Is the Treatment Center an Acute-Care Facility?

Acute inpatient treatment in a hospital setting is available for people with psychiatric emergencies. This period of hospitalization is usually short-term, lasting from a period of a few days to several months. Of course, there are different kinds of emergencies, and different ways for people to arrive at an acute-care facility.

The man who shoots himself in a suicide attempt will probably be taken first to a hospital emergency room. From there he may be transferred to a medical or surgical ward. Once he is physically stabilized, he should be carefully evaluated from a psychiatric standpoint for the underlying illness that led to the suicide attempt. Then, he will most likely be transferred either to the hospital's own psychiatric unit or to a specialized psychiatric hospital.

The woman whose life is in turmoil because of dependency on alcohol or drugs may make her own arrangements to be admitted to a psychiatric ward or a psychiatric hospital, or perhaps the therapist she is seeing will arrange for her to be hospitalized. In all probability she will be placed in a unit that deals exclusively with chemical dependency problems.

The delinquent adolescent boy—frequently with arrests on charges of drug abuse, theft to support the drug abuse behavior, or assaults—represents a significant disruptive force to a family. If he is clearly out of control, unmanageable at home, and a threat to himself or others, he may be referred directly to a facility that specializes in treating young people who have behavioral difficulties.

A teenage girl suffering from anorexia nervosa may diet to the point where she is literally starving and the situation is life-threatening. Although this behavior is beyond her control, she will often deny that anything is wrong. Hospitalization may be necessary, and the struggle between the adolescent and her parents may represent an initial conflict, although a most important first step, in seeking appropriate treatment. There are several programs designed specifically for the treatment of eating disorders. Personnel at these programs are valuable resources of information about this very serious illness.

If a young person suddenly becomes psychotic (what some people call a "nervous breakdown"), his parents, in their confusion and fear, may call the police—particularly if the psychotic episode takes the form of violence or uncontrollable rage and threats of physical harm. Trained police officers who recognize psychotic behavior can usually facilitate the referral of a disturbed person to a hospital emergency room. From there the patient can be admitted to a psychiatric ward if that is indicated.

A chronic schizophrenic patient sometimes functions relatively well for weeks or months, and then suffers a relapse into psychosis. If the patient's family realizes that a relapse is occurring, they may take her directly to the psychiatric hospital where she was previously treated.

When Is Hospitalization Necessary?

According to Doctors Peter E. Sifneos and William E. Greenberg in the *New Harvard Guide to Psychiatry*, there are four major factors that should determine whether the patient will be hospitalized in an acute-care facility. These factors are:

1. Protection: Hospitalization provides a considerable degree of protection against a patient's self-destructive behaviors, or against destructive actions directed toward others.
2. Containment: Some patients may not be self-destructive or destructive, but may be so overcome by their disorder that their ability to function is severely limited. For these patients, such as acutely depressed, psychotic or agitated individuals, hospitalization bestows the protection necessary for successful treatment.
3. Intensive or rapid diagnostic evaluation: Hospitalization allows maximum observation of the patient, and use of sophisticated diagnostic techniques not easily available outside the hospital.
4. Initiation of supervised treatment: Some patients because of co-existing physical problems (such as a cardiac condition) may benefit from treatment commencing in a controlled environment. In a hospital, any adverse reactions to treatment may be promptly dealt with.

Does the Facility Have Detoxification or Psychiatric Evaluation Facilities?

When a patient enters an acute-care facility under the influence of drugs, or in drug withdrawal, a detoxification program can be essential to the patient's ultimate recovery. In fact, many treatment specialists consider effective therapy almost impossible unless all mood-altering drugs have been "washed out" of the patient's system. This detoxification period requires special attention by treatment providers well-versed in helping patients through this most difficult and crucial time.

Similarly, a dedicated psychiatric evaluation may prove absolutely essential to establish the correct diagnosis. Many psychiatric and physical conditions have confusing and overlapping symptoms: an apparently "depressed" patient may really be suffering from undiagnosed cancer; a "panic disorder" patient may actually have a physical disorder called temporal lobe epilepsy. Facilities with dedicated evaluation programs are frequently best able to make the most accurate diagnosis.

Does the Facility Use "Locked Doors"?

Control is the one goal of inpatient hospital treatment. As the patient demonstrates increased ability to control his/her own behavior, he is accordingly given increasing opportunity to demonstrate that ability. It is because of this that you might see both locked and unlocked units in a psychiatric hospital. The locked unit is indicated when the patient is "out of control" and needs well-established boundaries. The unlocked unit may well be indicated when the patient is at a point at which he can accept structure and use it effectively. Some acutely disturbed patients actually feel more secure in response to a locked unit. The psychiatric program has the responsibility of caring for and protecting the patient. I have often explained to patients that I believe the locks on doors are to keep others outside. In any event, decisions should be made that insure utilization of the least restrictive environment which will safely care for the patient.

Are Laboratory Tests Used?

From the standpoint of doctors and nurses who are responsible for treatment, one big advantage of hospitalization is the ease of being able to conduct a full and comprehensive evaluation of the patient. It is an opportunity to carefully observe the patient over a 24-hour period of time. It also facilitates doing appropriate psychological and laboratory tests in a controlled, efficient, and coordinated manner. Finally, it is an ideal setting in which to carefully adjust the medication regimen while monitoring the results, as well as observing for development of side effects.

Why the emphasis on laboratory work? There are three main reasons:

1. Laboratory tests can help establish a medical diagnosis. If a patient is severely depressed, the depression may be "endogenous"—that is, caused by a biochemical imbalance unrelated to any identifiable physical ailment—or it may be a byproduct of a distinct disease, such as hypothyroidism, Huntington's disease, or cancer.

2. Much of modern-day psychiatric treatment involves medication, as well as talking or behavior therapy. Monitoring blood levels of a medication is often the best way to determine the ideal dosage for a particular patient. There's tremendous variation in the way different patients respond to a given medication. In addition, the same patient may respond differently to a medication at different times, depending on his general physical state and on what other medicines he's taking. For these reasons, a responsible physician likes to base dosage decisions on objective measurements whenever possible.

3. Toxicology screening can let the physician know whether the patient is surreptitiously taking street drugs or medications that aren't part of the treatment regimen. Although many hospitalized psychiatric patients sincerely want to be helped and do everything they can to comply with the prescribed therapy, a few feel compelled to "do their own thing." For example, some patients may coax or bribe visitors to bring them alcohol, barbiturates, or cocaine. In one hospital, a depressed woman was found to have an unusually per-

sistent and dangerous electrolyte imbalance. Nurses eventually discovered that this patient, who was obsessed with weight control, was a habitual abuser of diuretic pills and had brought the pills with her to the hospital. Such self-medication naturally interferes with the treatment process. If the physician in charge has doubts, results of blood or urine testing may help confirm or allay his suspicions.

Does the Facility Provide Counseling for Patients' Families?

Increasingly, family members of psychiatric patients are being encouraged to enter therapy for themselves. Therapists have discovered through experience that a sick spouse, child, or sibling can disrupt the functioning of the entire family system. The "well" people in the family may bear a considerable burden of anger, guilt, or frustration that they aren't even aware of. In family therapy, they learn how to cope with their relative's illness and how to reverse some of the negative effects this illness has had on their lives. This is frequently an integral part of the outlined treatment program in a hospital setting. Close communication with the patient's own doctor is facilitated, and visits can take place conveniently before or after the family therapy session.

Psychiatric patients who are graduating from acute care need a clearly defined follow-up plan. Again, the consolidation of services makes it possible for the doctor, one or more therapists, and a social worker to decide together with the patient on an appropriate, workable aftercare plan.

Is the Facility a Residential Treatment Center?

Residential treatment centers often look like private schools on sprawling, beautiful campuses in the countryside. In fact, some originally *were* private schools, founded in the early 1900s as "work camps" with accommodations for anywhere from fifty to one hundred affluent but delinquent adolescents.

Through the years they evolved, and by the 1940s many of them were staffed with psychiatrists.

Residential settings are seen as "stepdown" levels of care; however, there are specific needs for this longer and less intensive setting.

Residential care proves very useful in the treatment of adolescents. Some of today's well-known, sophisticated residential treatment facilities were originally "homes" or orphanages sponsored by religious groups. Gradually, as the children's needs were identified, the emphasis shifted from mere custodial care to appropriate psychiatric treatment.

The same concept has also been applied successfully, although to a lesser extent, in responding to the needs of certain groups of adults. Some residential centers are designed for the care and treatment of mentally retarded people, others for alcohol and drug abusers, and still others for patients with schizophrenia.

From the concept of group homes which provide full-time care, there arose further "stepdowns" such as halfway houses. This name reflects the time the resident is expected to spend in the treatment setting, while using the rest of the day out in the community. The programs provide supportive care while the resident begins to re-enter society and the workplace, assuming increasing levels of responsibility for himself. Support comes in the form of a structured, supervised living arrangement, the companionship of other people working toward similar goals, and the availability of professional counseling.

You may have heard or read about some of the well-known therapeutic communities, such as Phoenix House, Daytop Village, Odyssey, and Ariba. The philosophy of these communities favors dealing with personal problems through encounter-group techniques, including a good deal of confrontation. The theory is that addicts learn best from other addicts, who can see through their denial and defense mechanisms. Used in the right way, confrontation can indeed prove to be a powerful and influential treatment force.

Is the Facility a Halfway House?

Much smaller than a residential treatment center, the typical halfway house may accommodate an average of only fourteen residents. There are halfway houses for alcoholics and drug addicts, and also for schizophrenics in remission. Please note that a halfway house usually accepts only one category of recovering patient. In other words, a house that accommodates recovering alcoholics or drug abusers will not be interested in taking on a recovering schizophrenic as a resident. This is understandable because the treatment program is targeted for a particular group.

Almost always, halfway house residents are adults who have functioned on their own before psychiatric treatment and who expect to function on their own again. They may be college-age students in their early twenties, or much older individuals who have had careers and raised families. In most cases their lives have been shattered emotionally or financially as a result of their illness, and they need help getting back on their feet and functioning as productive citizens again.

The halfway house provides structure and discipline through well-enforced house rules. Men and women residents have strictly separate sleeping quarters, and in some cases separate dining quarters, too. Socializing, although permitted, is highly regulated. The residents have to be up and out of bed by a certain hour of the morning, and back in bed by a set time at night. Meals are taken on a well-defined schedule. Each resident must have a job in the community, and must contribute some of each paycheck to the halfway house for room and board. Good living and work habits are structured to help the residents prepare for resumption of the responsibilities for themselves in the near future.

In most parts of the country there are not nearly enough halfway houses to meet current needs; long waiting lists, unfortunately, are common. Establishing a new halfway house takes money and time. If the house is to be located in an already developed community, there may be intense resistance from unsympathetic neighbors who imagine that the residents might be disruptive or violent.

Ten Questions to Ask About Any Treatment Program

1. Is an experienced medical doctor in charge?
2. Does the program provide a total treatment environment (including individual, group, and family therapy)?
3. Is there a fully qualified staff (including psychiatrists, psychologists, nurses, and social workers) available?
4. Does the program use effective diagnostic and laboratory tests to help make correct diagnoses, and to evaluate treatment?
5. Does the program provide for family sessions and counseling when necessary? If so, how many family sessions are there?
6. For child and adolescent hospital programs: does the program offer an accredited school and/or vocational training to prevent children and teens from falling behind in their schoolwork?
7. Are family members encouraged to visit?
8. Are support groups, such as Alcoholics Anonymous, encouraged?
9. Does the program provide well-defined aftercare (through individual or group therapy) for long-term treatment?
10. How much does the program cost? Will your insurance cover all or part of the treatment, and for how long will your insurance continue?

Outpatient Care

This minimally restrictive form of treatment, suitable for patients capable of living at home while receiving treatment, comes in various forms:

Outpatients in the day program or partial hospitalization program of a psychiatric hospital live at home in the evenings and on weekends, and spend their weekdays at the hospital instead of going to work or school. Their daily schedule will depend on their needs and capabilities.

A schizophrenic patient who is doing well on medication but who can't handle an outside job may spend several hours a day in the program's sheltered workshop. She may also be scheduled for vocational training, occupational therapy, music, dance, or art therapy. She'll be seen regularly by a psychiatrist, and she may have a session with a counselor daily or several times a week.

An alcoholic patient who has taken a leave of absence from work may be able to attend intensive daily educational and training sessions at a hospital or clinic, while still living at home with his family. A decade ago, virtually all hospital-based recovery programs for alcoholics and drug abusers were inpatient programs. Since then, day programs have sprung up throughout the country and are proving to be popular and successful. Several well-structured studies support that some patients do very well in these settings. Day programs are far less costly than inpatient programs. This is important, when appropriate, because of the need to constantly be sensitive to the concepts of the least restrictive environment and cost containment.

Outpatients in an evening program are free to work or go to school as usual. They attend their evening group sessions at the clinic as if they were enrolled in a night school. An evening outpatient program is an excellent form of aftercare for people who have successfully completed either a day program or a period of psychiatric hospitalization. It reinforces the new habits they learned during intensive therapy, and keeps them in contact with others who have similar goals.

Obviously, patients who see a psychiatrist or other therapist once or several times a week are also in a level of outpatient care.

Support Groups

Alcoholics Anonymous (AA) is the grandparent of support programs, which now number in the hundreds. A support group is an association of nonprofessionals who share a common problem or concern. Therefore, it's not a type of psychiatric treatment per se. However, I am including support groups in this list because they provide a valuable aftercare service for people who have been through hospital-based psychiatric treatment. Many very reputable hospitals who treat people for alcohol and drug dependency firmly direct patients to become active members of AA or NA (Narcotics Anonymous) even before graduating from the hospital program.

Groups such as Drug Anonymous, Gamblers Anonymous, and Overeaters Anonymous offer help to those who are personally afflicted with a compulsion or an illness. Other groups reach out to the families and loved ones of ill or troubled people: Al-Anon, for relatives and friends of alcoholics; Nar-Anon, for parents and siblings of drug abusers; Families Anonymous, for families of schizophrenic patients. There are support groups for relatives of patients with cancer, for people who have lost a spouse, for manic-depressive patients, for parents who have lost a child, for women recovering from a mastectomy . . . the list is large and still growing.

Support groups do a great deal of good. Not only do they focus on a particular emotional concern, but they also provide a network of compassionate friends. Membership in a support group eases the isolation and loneliness of people who may have spent many years in solitary struggle with a problem they mistakenly thought was theirs alone.

Support groups do have limitations: patients suffering from a severe psychiatric disorder, or from a physical condition masquerading as a psychiatric condition, will receive little benefit if support groups are the sole source of treatment. Their specific psychiatric needs will require attention as well. But I believe that support groups, when used properly, can help many people recover from their psychiatric disorder and should be considered an adjunct to a comprehensive treatment plan.

One word of advice: if you're interested in joining a support group, it may be helpful to visit several and decide with which you feel most comfortable. This kind of comparative shopping is quite possible with the more widespread support groups, such as AA and NA. For example, a drug-abusing teenager who has just come through a hospital detoxification and rehabilitation program may want to affiliate with a young people's AA or NA meeting, not an adult meeting.

5

EVALUATING YOUR TREATMENT

How do patients evaluate their treatment? How do they know if they—or a family member or loved one—are getting the best treatment? And if there is a problem with treatment, does the problem lie with the patient or therapist? Is it time for a change of therapy and therapist, or should the patient modify his or her attitude toward therapy?

As a starting point for our discussion, let's assume you are the patient and that you have been seeing a therapist (either a psychiatrist, psychologist, or social worker) in private, once-a-week sessions. What complaints might you have, and how legitimate are such complaints? Let's look at a few.

"My therapist is cold and unfeeling." Presumably most professional therapists chose that line of work because of their genuine concern and deep feeling for other people. Of course, there are many ways of expressing interest and concern. If your personality is warm, emotional, and vibrant, what will be the outcome if you happen to have chosen a therapist who is by nature somewhat aloof and reserved? It's possible that the two of you will never really hit it off. On the other hand, the therapist's cool rationality may be just what you need to help you see your life from a new perspective.

What if your therapist is actually rude or abrasive—fails to greet you politely at the beginning of a session, doesn't react when you share an emotionally charged thought, makes uncomplimentary or critical comments, cancels appointments or reschedules them for a different time without apologizing or asking your permission? This type of behavior, quite uncharacteristic of the skilled professional, may be an indication that you do indeed need to find a different therapist. Your therapist should treat you courteously and respectfully, as if you were a welcome guest. Don't settle for less!

Some therapists are afraid to act too friendly toward a patient, for fear of crossing an invisible barrier that separates professional relationships from social ones. It's true that a professional relationship sets limits on closeness and requires a degree of restraint. However, professionalism does not preclude kindness. As a patient, you want very much to see your therapist as a friend—that is, as someone who is strongly on your side, allied with you in a common struggle. By that definition, the professional relationship can certainly include friendship.

"My therapist intimidates me." If you're like most people, you were probably nervous the first time you met with a therapist. You knew you were expected to share intimate details of your life. You weren't sure how serious your symptoms were, and you were somewhat afraid to find out. You were nervous about the label the therapist would pin on you— were you normal, disturbed, or truly "crazy"?

A skillful therapist will try to put you at ease at the start of the first session—asking you if you found your way to the office without difficulty, for instance, or inquiring about the temperature outside. Nevertheless, your tensions and anxieties probably won't dissolve entirely even if the therapist is relaxed and helpful. You will be thinking and talking about things you find disturbing—that's what you're there for!—and in the process of probing repressed, emotionally charged thoughts, you may grope for words, misuse words, stutter, or make completely uncharacteristic mistakes in grammar and pronunciation. All this is normal and understandable. Don't let it fluster you.

Occasionally a patient finds she's "frozen" in the therapist's presence, and can't do anything but cry uncontrollably throughout the entire session. This may be a manifestation of a dynamic called transference: the patient's tendency to "see" someone else in the therapist—her authoritarian and frightening father, for instance—and to interact as though the therapist really were that other person. It's up to the therapist to recognize transference and help the patient overcome it. If many sessions come and go with no progress beyond the "frozen" stage, the transference problem isn't being dealt with adequately.

"My therapist and I don't see eye-to-eye." Oddly enough, even if you really want therapy you may use various unconscious maneuvers to obstruct its progress. This very common phenomenon of resistance to therapy is rooted in fears of losing whatever emotional defenses you've managed to construct over the years.

Resistance to therapy can take the form of annoyance with the therapist's personal characteristics. You may feel you can't stand the way the therapist dresses, pronounces certain words, or wiggles his eyebrows. If this is the case, try to sort out in your own mind whether these personal quirks are really so important that they're undermining the therapy, or whether you're seizing on them as diversions from the real therapy work you need to do.

Resistance may also show up as unreasonable suspicion about what the therapist is going to do with all the personal information you divulge. Therapists have very high standards of confidentiality and will not even reveal your *name* to an inquirer—for instance, a prospective employer—without your consent. However, for your own peace of mind you should have a talk about this with your own therapist.

Another form of resistance is a fear that the therapist will somehow brainwash you to give up your chosen philosophy of life. If you feel even slightly concerned about "losing your identity," you and your therapist should have a conversation about the goals you want to establish for yourself.

Of course, a clash in fundamental philosophy may not be a form of resistance at all, but a serious obstacle to therapy.

If you have strong feminist tendencies and your therapist is firmly convinced that a woman's only place is in the home, it's probably time to look for another therapist. Ditto if you're deeply devout and your therapist scoffs openly at religion, or if you're militantly gay and your therapist believes homosexuality is a perversion. The therapeutic alliance may be flexible, but it does have its elastic limit! Your therapist's orientation on such issues should not be the focus of therapy. It's you and your orientations which take precedent.

"My therapist doesn't listen to me." Ideally, the therapist should give you an entire session of undivided attention. But maybe that's not what's happening. It's possible for a therapist to become inadvertently inattentive, especially after seeing several patients in a row. Maybe he will yawn, look at his watch, stare off into space, close his eyes, or ask you a question that you've just answered. There may be overly frequent phone interruptions. You don't have to feel guilty or stifle your annoyance if your therapist doesn't seem to be focusing his entire attention on you. Share your concern with him. He may not have realized that his mind was wandering, and he may be able to take steps to minimize this tendency in the future: keeping the consultation room well ventilated and comfortably cool, getting enough exercise and sleep to feel alert, eating lightly at midday to avoid afternoon drowsiness. If his reaction is angry and defensive, that's a trouble signal.

A few impatient therapists go to the opposite extreme: they're so intensely involved in the session and so eager to reach a diagnosis that they interrupt the patient in midsentence or try to put words in his mouth. Obviously, this kind of hustle is an impediment to effective therapy. If you feel your therapist is rushing you, it's important to tell him so. A sensitive and competent professional will back off and let you take more of the initiative.

"My therapist talks down to me." You may have gone to your first therapy session with a list of things that bothered you and that you thought were problems for you. Perhaps you used as many psychological terms as you could, to let the therapist know you were intelligent and had done your homework. The therapist may have surprised or even wounded you by asking you to stop using jargon.

Every medical specialty, including psychiatry, has its set of technical terms. Unfortunately, these terms sometimes generate more heat than light, even among the professionals themselves. Because jargon can oversimplify and dehumanize a problem, your therapist can get to know you better by hearing you talk about your thoughts and emotions in your own words. If you feel intense anger toward your mother, just say so—don't assume you'll make a better impression by talking about your "Oedipal conflict."

There's another side to this story. If your therapist does use a technical word or phrase, she owes you a full explanation of what it means. It is very frustrating to receive a fancy-sounding diagnosis—for example, "unipolar depression"—without a clear and thorough definition of the term. If your therapist peppers her talk with jargon and doesn't explain the terms even when you ask her to, then she really is not effectively communicating with you.

"I'm in love with my therapist." Watch out for this trap! Psychotherapy deals in intense feelings and personal revelations, and this can foster a hothouse emotional climate between patient and therapist. Since romantic feelings toward the therapist may actually be one form of *resistance* to therapy (i.e., a diversion tactic that allows the patient to avoid dealing with unpleasant emotional issues), it's necessary to confront, explore, and resolve such feelings so the therapy can progress.

Although your therapist should consider sexual contact with patients strictly taboo—for both psychological and legal reasons—it helps if you consciously adopt the same attitude. That way, if romantic impulses between you and the therapist do happen to emerge during therapy, both of you will be in a strong position to deal with the impulses objectively and put them in their proper perspective. Fortunately, analyzing such feelings almost always reduces their intensity.

When the person in Treatment Is a Family Member or Loved One

Next we should consider some questions that may arise when the person who's receiving treatment is not you but rather your spouse, parent, or child. If you're the one paying for the treatment, you'll want to make sure you're getting fair value for your dollar. Even if you have nothing to do with the financial aspect of therapy, you'll want to assure yourself that your loved one is getting the best help available. Nevertheless, this doesn't entitle you to "reports" of the therapy, or details about the process. Therapy is impeded and compromised if the patient fears there will be a breach in confidentiality. It is necessary for the patient to request and agree about contacts between the therapist and significant others. Don't lose sight of the fact that the therapist is working to help the *patient*—not the patient's family or friends.

"My child's therapist doesn't give any medications." Over the past thirty years, the array of psychoactive medications has expanded considerably (see Chapter 3). Many disorders that were formerly treated only by talk therapy can now be dealt with through a combination of medication, behavior modification, and talking. Note that this does not mean there is a magic pill for every mental or emotional problem! If your child is in therapy and isn't receiving any kind of medication, there are a number of possible reasons why:

1. Your child's illness does not lend itself to treatment with medication.
2. The therapist is not a psychiatrist, and therefore has no license to prescribe medications.
3. The therapist is a psychiatrist whose orientation dictates a conservative approach to the use of medication for children.

If you yourself are uncomfortable with the idea of "drugs for the mind," then you may be very satisfied with a talk-only therapist, particularly if your child seems to be responding well to treatment. It's a good idea to have an open discussion with your therapist about your feelings on this important issue. On the other hand, your resistance to medication may be impeding your child's progress. Consequently, if you don't think your child is responding to talk therapy alone, you may want to broach this topic with the therapist, or seek a second opinion.

"My husband doesn't take his medicine regularly." Failing to go along with a prescribed medication regimen is known as noncompliance, and is one of the most common problems in psychiatry. There are several quite understandable reasons for noncompliance:

1. The medication may cause unpleasant side effects. Some medications cause side effects in almost all patients; others cause untoward effects in only a small percentage of people who take them.
2. Patients often forget to take their medication once they're feeling better. We're all familiar with this phenomenon: we take the antibiotic faithfully as long as our throat is still sore, but once the soreness vanishes, we get very casual about finishing up the bottle of pills as we were told.
3. People may resist taking medication every day of their lives because it reminds them of something they would rather forget—namely, that they suffer from a chronic disorder. This is another example of the *denial* we mentioned earlier.

Just because noncompliance is understandable, however, doesn't mean it is not a problem. If your husband doesn't like to take his antidepressant medication because it makes him feel nervous and jittery, it's important that he tell this to the doctor who gave him the prescription. It may be that adjustment of the dosage, changes in the time for taking the pill, or a change to an alternative medication will help. There is a wide range of antidepressants, and it's very possible that a different one would not cause those unpleasant jittery feelings. If he's taking lithium to prevent manic episodes and often misses doses out of sheer forgetfulness, you and he together may be able to devise a system of reminders. If he refuses to take lithium over the long term because he doesn't believe he needs it, you should make sure his therapist knows this. In the event that he does enter a manic phase again, the therapist will be able to point out to him that this probably happened because of noncompliance.

"In spite of therapy, my aging mother's mind is getting worse instead of better." It's very hard to watch a healthy, functioning adult slowly deteriorate as old age takes over. Even painful physical decline may seem trivial compared to the mental regression that robs the individual of her memory and capacity to reason. "Senility" has many causes, only some of which are treatable with our present state of knowledge. Even with the finest care, some old people seem to reach a stage where they lose their mental faculties, sometimes quite rapidly.

It's a mistake, however, to consider *all* such deterioration inevitable. One common problem is overmedication. If your mother is being treated in a nursing home, it's possible that she is being given sedatives and sleeping medication inappropriately. Another common problem results from interactions of different medications. Medications that independently may not cause side effects may cause significant problems when taken together. A consultation with a competent and concerned psychiatrist may result in orders for less medication, or for different medications less likely to cause an adverse interaction. Sometimes, a simple change or adjustment in dosage will be enough to restore a person's mental state.

Unrecognized depression is another potential problem in elderly people. What looks like dullness, apathy, and memory loss may actually be signs of major depression. Growing old carries its own special load of stress: surviving the loss of a spouse and of many dear friends, living on a reduced income, coping with a sense of being unnecessary and superfluous in the world. Many older people suffer psychologically because they're no longer able to care for themselves independently.

Often people, including elderly parents, may neglect or hesitate to mention feelings of depression to their physician.

Any sign of depression, or any other mental disorder, should always be brought to the attention of their physician.

"My loved one's therapy doesn't seem to be going anywhere." As with yourself, you should consider taking action on behalf of your ill family member if there seems to have been no progress in therapy for a long time. The simplest strategy is to make sure that both patient and therapist agree on the goals they've set for therapy. Sometimes a restatement of those goals is all it takes to nudge the course of therapy back on track. On the other hand, if the patient and the therapist seem poles apart in what they consider reasonable and desirable goals, that's an indication that it's time to reassess the treatment plan and possibly seek out another treatment option.

SECTION II

COMMON PSYCHIATRIC DIAGNOSES

This section describes several psychiatric syndromes. The resource for much of the following material is the *Diagnostic and Statistical Manual of Mental Disorders* (3rd Edition-Revised)—frequently referred to as DSM-III-R. DSM-III-R is an official action of the American Psychiatric Association, and it sets forth for the psychiatric profession the current thinking about how to categorize and describe various psychiatric conditions. (As the Introduction to DSM-III-R puts it, soon after the previous edition—DSM-III—was published, "it became widely accepted in the United States as the common language of mental health clinicians and researchers for communicating about the disorders for which they have professional responsibility.")

In addition to DSM-III-R, however, this book also draws on many other sources, and it has been prepared not for the mental health professional but for the untrained nonprofessional who desires a greater understanding of mental disorders and their treatment. As such, this book is not an authorized version of DSM-III-R or any other work and the responsibility for its contents rests with its author and editors.

This section discusses only a sampling of the many mental

disorders that have been identified by the psychiatric profession. Also, it is not intended to serve as a substitute for the advice and treatment of a competent clinician; instead, its purpose is to give its readers a greater awareness and understanding of the conditions described here. Readers who wish further information, or who believe they could benefit from professional care, should consult an appropriate mental health professional.

6

DISORDERS THAT MAY
FIRST APPEAR IN INFANCY,
CHILDHOOD, OR ADOLESCENCE

Condition: Autistic Disorder

Also known as infantile autism and Kanner's syndrome, this is the most severe form of a condition known as Pervasive Developmental Disorder. It involves repetitive, stereotyped activity; very limited interests; and an inability to communicate and interact with other people and to think imaginatively.

Background

Autistic disorder, which occurs in 4 or 5 children out of every 10,000, begins in infancy or childhood and usually persists throughout life. It is 3 or 4 times more common in boys than in girls. The cause is unknown. Formerly, it was thought that parents were to blame for causing this condition in their children. Autistic disorder is now thought to be a form of brain dysfunction. Factors sometimes linked with its development include rubella (German measles) in the mother during pregnancy, lack of oxygen during birth, encephalitis, and infantile spasms.[1]

Often the autistic person is also mentally retarded. However, even severely mentally retarded people are usually sociable and able to communicate either verbally or nonverbally. Autistic people, by contrast, take no interest or pleasure in social contacts.

An autistic adult may have many of the negative symptoms seen in residual-phase schizophrenia: social withdrawal, peculiar behavior, absent or inappropriate emotions, and odd use of language. By definition, however, autism begins in childhood, whereas schizophrenia usually develops in adolescence or adulthood.

Symptoms

The diagnosis of autistic disorder is made only when a child functions very abnormally (for his or her age) in three areas: social interaction, communication, and activities/interest.

Social interaction abnormalities must include at least two of the following items:

- No appreciation that other people have feelings
- No impulse to seek comfort from other people when in distress
- No tendency to imitate others (i.e., waving bye-bye); or inappropriate imitation at the wrong times
- No simple playing with others
- No interest in making friends; or no notion of how to act friendly

Communication abnormalities must include at least one of the following (later items are more likely to be seen in older individuals):

---

[1]"infantile spasms"—source: DSM-III-R p37 2nd full paragraph (beginning "Predisposing factors") 2nd sentence.

- No attempt to communicate by cooing, chattering, pointing, or making faces
- Stiff, unfriendly body language; staring off into space when in a group; no eye contact; no greeting or smiling
- No playacting or imaginary play; no interest in make-believe stories
- Odd way of using the voice: speaking in a high pitch or a monotone, or making statements sound like questions
- Mechanically repeating what someone else says; using "you" instead of "I" when talking about self; mixing up parts of speech; disrupting a conversation with irrelevant remarks

Activity/interest abnormalities must include at least one of the following:

- Repetitive, stereotyped movements such as flicking the hand, banging the head, or spinning in a circle
- Preoccupation with smelling or feeling parts of objects; or having an attachment to a string, a nail, or some other non-cuddly object
- Severe, undue distress when something is moved from its usual place
- Insistence on adhering strictly to precise, rigid routines
- Obsession with a single narrow interest, such as lining things up or collecting facts about the weather

Treatment

There is no well-established treatment for the behavioral abnormalities of autistic disorder. Some of the complications of autism can be treated, however. About 25 percent of autistic people have seizures at some point. Some autistic teenagers and adults are partly aware of, and depressed by, their social handicaps. Stress can cause catatonia, or delusions and hallucinations, in autistic individuals. The seizures, depression, and psychosis may be treated with medication.

Condition: Mental Retardation

This term describes intellectual functioning that is significantly below normal. Retardation begins before the age of 18 and impedes the ability to live independently and interact with others in society.

Background

There are 6 million retarded people in the United States; males outnumber females 3:2. As measured by IQ tests (a "normal" IQ is 90 to 110), about 85 percent of those affected are mildly retarded; another 10 percent are moderately retarded.

Retardation can result from different factors: heredity; a genetic defect; a disease such as German measles; poisons such as lead; or even social factors (poverty, malnutrition). A pregnant woman who takes illicit drugs or eats a poor diet may ruin the fetus's developing brain. Some experts see retardation primarily as a biological disease; others consider it to be a social problem.

Many retarded people can lead full, productive lives. But coping with retardation is made more difficult because of its social stigma. Patients may have trouble finding professional help or the services they need to live independently. Some retarded individuals are all but abandoned by their families, who can't deal with the emotional and financial burden of caring for a chronically needy person.

Is retardation "incurable"? The fact that 3 percent of the population of children are affected compared to only 1 percent of adults shows that, properly managed, mental ability can rise. Furthermore, 95 out of 100 retarded people live outside of hospitals, showing that they are able to handle the physical and emotional challenges that confront them.

The stigma often associated with mental retardation suggests that the condition is a "tragedy." However, this need not be the case. Many retarded individuals, if they get the structure and support they need, prove to be loving, caring, and dependable. If we refuse to take the time to discover this, we deprive ourselves of an important, enriching experience.

Symptoms

Severity	IQ	Traits
Mild	50-69	Adults function at sixth-grade level; "childlike" behavior; normal speech but poor command of factual information. Often self-supporting, but may need special help in times of stress.
Moderate	35-49	Function at second-grade level. Poor speech (lisps, etc); need training to learn how to dress, wash, and feed themselves. May be able to do limited, unskilled tasks under supervision. Emotions are simple and obvious. Many live in the community in group homes where there is constant supervision.
Severe	20-39	Preschool: poor muscle development and control; no speech. School-age: some speech; may learn basic hygiene (use of toilet, etc); may read a few words. As adults, can do simple jobs (such as drying dishes) under supervision.
Profound	Below 20	Oblivious to others; speech may be absent; require feeding, constant supervision.

Treatment

For many retarded people, behavioral therapy offers the greatest hope for improving the day-to-day skills needed to survive, including good eating and hygiene habits. It also deals with self-destructive or aggressive behavior and offers ways to cope with fears and thus reduce anxiety.

Psychotherapy may be of some value for mildly retarded persons. The emphasis is on helping patients resolve conflicts by expressing their feelings. This can be important, because many people—including some health-care professionals—tend to forget that the retarded *do* have feelings.

Medications can be used to treat specific symptoms in some mentally retarded patients. Lithium may act to control aggressive behavior, and beta-blockers such as propranolol may reduce self-destructive behavior.

Condition: Attention-deficit Hyperactivity Disorder (ADHD)

A childhood disorder characterized by short attention span, poor concentration, impulsivity, and ceaseless activity. Sometimes known as attention-deficit disorder, or ADD.

Background

The features of ADHD were first described in 1926 by a physician who noticed the symptoms in his own young son. Over the years the diagnosis was broadly applied to describe children whom we would not now recognize as meeting the criteria for this diagnosis. Recently the condition was redefined to restrict its use to describe children who fit a certain pattern of behavior (see "Symptoms," below).

ADHD, seen in perhaps 3 percent of children, is three to nine times more common in boys than in girls. About half of the cases first occur before age 4. Many times ADHD isn't noticed until the child begins attending school.

There's no known cause for the disorder, although one theory is that an abnormality in the central nervous system, such as the buildup of certain poisons, may predispose a child to develop it. Neurological diseases such as cerebral palsy or epilepsy contribute to ADHD in some cases. Social factors such as child abuse or neglect and a disorganized or chaotic home life may also play a role. Frequently, the parents of an ADHD child have abused alcohol, or have conduct disorders of their own or antisocial personalities.

The behavior problems associated with ADHD can disrupt a young person's life. Typically a child with the disorder does poorly in school and has trouble interacting socially with others. Poor performance or social isolation leads to low self-esteem, changes in mood, low frustration tolerance, and outbursts of temper. Some aspects of the disorder—low concentration, for example—may persist into adulthood. Today's ADHD child is at risk of becoming tomorrow's conduct-disordered adolescent or antisocial adult.

Symptoms

Restlessness (fidgeting, squirming, difficulty staying seated), impatience (can't wait for his turn during a game, shouts out answers to a teacher's question, interrupts or intrudes on others), inability to concentrate (doesn't listen, doesn't follow through on tasks or play activities, switches quickly from one unfinished activity to another, loses things), agitation (has trouble playing quietly, talks too much), hyperactivity (excessive movement, often rapid but usually with a purpose, "always on the go"), tendency to do dangerous things such as running into the street.

ADHD, which strikes before age 7 but may be detected as early as age 2, is considered severe if many of the possible symptoms are present and the child's ability to function at home, at school, and with friends is impaired.

Treatment

Psychostimulant medications, which in adults act as stimulants, actually help hyperactive children maintain their attention. These medications, such as methylphenidate (Ritalin), do not themselves change children's behavior; rather, when prescribed correctly, they allow children to control their impulses. In addition, these medications facilitate the use of other treatment strategies, such as psychotherapy (see below). Although studies definitely proving that these medications work in ADHD are lacking, most psychiatrists report clinical success when using these psychostimulants.

While controversy exists about use of these medications, most child psychiatrists have found them to be both safe and effective when administered correctly. Unfortunately, some physicians not sensitive to child psychiatry issues have prescribed these medications inappropriately. Most psychiatrists believe that medications are most effective when they are part of a broad-based treatment approach that includes psychotherapy for both the child and the parents.

Psychotherapy helps hyperactive children explore their feelings and motivations and helps them find other ways of dealing with frustration. The behavioral approach helps them develop ways of anticipating and, hopefully, controlling their behavior. By working with the schools, therapists can help teachers set reasonable goals for schoolwork. This reduces the child's frustration level and enhances self-esteem. Phenothiazines (a class of tranquilizers, including chlorpromazine) can help calm agitated people. Unfortunately, these drugs are sometimes used as "chemical straitjackets" to make a patient easier to control. Like all drugs, they have side effects, ranging from damage to the blood to development of severe body-movement disorders. It is for this reason that the patient should be followed at regular intervals by a clinician who is experienced with these agents. It is important that the clinician be able to notice side effects as soon as they appear, and make any needed adjustments to the dosage or the type of medication.

Condition: Conduct Disorder

A persistent pattern of disobedience or aggressive behavior toward others. The person with a conduct disorder frequently—and deliberately—violates the rights of others or oversteps the rules of society. There are three subtypes of conduct disorders. The solitary aggressive type involves aggressive behavior by an individual, while the group type involves such behavior with a group of peers, like a gang. The "undifferentiated" type—probably the majority—contains features of both of the other types.

Background

Between 10 and 15 out of every 100 young people seen in psychiatric clinics are thought to have some form of conduct disorder. Boys with the disorder outnumber girls by over 4 to 1. In males, the trouble usually begins before puberty, especially in the solitary type; in females with solitary disorder, onset usually follows puberty. The sooner it starts, the greater the likelihood that the disorder will persist into adulthood.

Because the symptoms overlap, it can sometimes be hard to distinguish a conduct disorder from attention-deficit hyperactivity disorder (see above) or a learning disability. People with conduct disorders experience a number of complications, ranging from trouble with the law, the effects of abusing illicit drugs, venereal disease, physical injury, and suicidal behavior. Their symptoms are often the result of various forms of delinquent behavior.

These are some tough customers—physically aggressive, cruel, without concern for the feelings of others, lacking guilt or remorse. Their crimes range from substance abuse, theft, and burglary to rape, arson—even murder. Although individuals may have loyalty for their "group" or gang, they may just as easily turn around and squeal on other members to save their own necks when they get into trouble.

Not surprisingly, many of these individuals—but not all—come from poor families, often without a strong father figure. Their homes are filled with instability, violence, punishment, substance abuse, and threats of abandonment. Sometimes brain damage, learning disabilities, or poor performance in school can trigger symptoms of the disorder.

Symptoms

Typically, a person with a conduct disorder does at least three of the following over the course of six months: steals, runs away from home overnight more than once, skips school or work, lies (for some reason other than avoiding a beating or sexual abuse), sets fires or otherwise destroys property, breaks into someone else's property, is cruel to animals or people, rapes, starts fights, and fights with a weapon more than once.

The condition is considered severe if the person engages in several of these activities or causes serious harm to another person or property.

Treatment

The sooner the disorder strikes, and the more severe the symptoms, the greater the chance that the troubled child will become a troubled adult. Treatment requires a carefully supervised combination of behavioral therapy, family therapy, specialized education, and sometimes the use of medications to reduce aggression.

In many cases it helps to hospitalize patients for a period of time. Hospitalization removes them from the environment that is contributing to their agitation, and provides a structured setting in which both staff and other youngsters can confront them about their conduct. In this structured environment, the successful program will insist that patients take increasing responsibility for their behavior and the need to change the way they act.

Condition: Oppositional Defiant Disorder

A pattern of negative, hostile, and defiant behavior. Oppositional behavior bears a "family resemblance" to a conduct disorder (see above) but involves a much less serious degree of violation of other people's rights and property.

Background

The disorder usually emerges between age 8 and early adolescence. The pattern is more commonly seen in boys, although after puberty the ratio of boys to girls is about equal. No one is really sure why the disorder arises or what might predispose a child to develop it.

Much of the oppositional behavior takes place in the home. Children argue with parents, swear, and throw tantrums. A request to take out the trash can launch an intense, screaming fight. Children are usually touchy, easily annoyed—and often annoying. If caught in a mistake, or if they get into trouble, they are quick to blame someone else for the problem. They don't see themselves as being unreasonable; instead, they claim they are victims of an unreasonable set of rules.

Naturally, much of this is a normal, if distressing, part of growing up; what makes it a disorder is essentially a matter of degree.

Interestingly, because children with the disorder tend to act out only against adults they know well, the misbehavior doesn't necessarily emerge in situations outside the home. The same child who is a pain in his parents' neck might be the teacher's prized pupil. Similarly, the disorder can be hard to diagnose since the child will show few signs of defiant behavior when being examined by a doctor.

Symptoms

Over a period of six months, a person with oppositional defiant disorder frequently engages in at least half of the following behaviors: fits of temper, arguments with adults, disobeying rules set by adults, ignoring assigned tasks, acting in a purposely annoying or provocative way, blaming others when he makes mistakes, using profanity, acting touchy or resentful, doing things to "get back" or "even the score."

The condition is considered severe if more than half of these behaviors are present and the person's relationships with peers and adults at home and at school are impaired.

Treatment

Some of the treatment techniques successful in the management of conduct disorder may be useful with oppositional defiant disorder. If the symptoms are disruptive and severe enough, a structured environment—a treatment program or a special type of school—may be useful. Once again, the goal is to confront the youngster effectively, so that he will accept responsibility for change and work to bring about positive changes.

Failure to deal with this appropriately during the formative years results in an adult with similar behavior. Understandably, society refuses to put up with an "oppositional defiant" adult; social and legal problems are likely to develop for this type of individual.

Condition: Anorexia Nervosa

Refusal to eat resulting in emaciation, exaggerated fear of fatness, distorted idea of what the body actually looks like, and reduced sexuality (absence of menstruation and reduction in breast size in women, reduced sexual drive in men).

Background

The first cases of self-starvation were reported over three hundred years ago; the name "anorexia nervosa" was first used around 1873. Actually, the term is a misnomer. Anorexia means "loss of appetite," but anorectic patients are actually hungry all the time.

Almost all anorectic patients—over 95 percent—are female. The disorder usually strikes in early adolescence and affects perhaps as many as one girl out of every hundred (some experts say the figure is closer to one out of eight hundred). Males who starve themselves are likely to be engaged in professions where thinness is a virtue—jockeys, dancers, and so on.

In many cases, starvation is a response to intense social pressure to be thin. It also represents a girl's way of fending off the changes wrought by puberty and she denies her developing sexuality. By starving herself, she sheds her femininity—body shape, breasts, menstruation—and thus delays making the transition into adolescence. It may also represent a misguided cry for attention, a misstep toward independence from family, a response to a stressful situation or personal loss, or an expression of a driven, perfectionist personality. Many anorectics claim their ability to starve themselves makes them "special," and that the people trying to cure them are robbing them of their unique identity.

Anorexia usually starts off as food restriction—cutting back to one meal a day, eating low-calorie foods, strenuous exercise, and so on. Starvation is hard to keep up, however. Patients often become so ravenously hungry that they succumb to the overwhelming urge to eat and go on a food binge. But the prospect of having all that food inside is too much to bear, and the anorectic will often get rid of the meal (purge it) by self-induced vomiting or the use of laxatives and diuretics. Thus anorexia can "slide" into another eating disorder known as bulimia nervosa (see below).

The end point of starvation is death, sometimes by suicide; the mortality rate of anorexia is between 5 and 18 percent. This is a serious and potentially life-threatening disease.

Symptoms

Body weight at least 15 percent less than what would normally be expected for the patient's age and height; fear of gaining weight even though severely thin; "feeling fat" despite emaciation; at least three skipped menstrual periods.

As their weight drops, patients become obsessed with

thoughts of food and eating. They engage in bizarre habits and rituals, such as cutting food into tiny cubes, eating inside a closet, and are frequently very controlling about food in their interactions with others. In order to lose more weight, they may exercise frantically. A gain of even an ounce can send them into a panic.

Many of the physical changes experienced in anorexia—extreme sensitivity to cold, slowing heartbeat, low blood pressure, and so on—are not directly caused by the disorder but are secondary to the starvation that anorexia produces.

Treatment

The first step is to restore the patient's weight, if not to its original level, then at least to the point where it is not life-threatening. This step often means hospitalization. Unless starvation is reversed, the patient can't benefit from any other form of treatment. It's important for her to understand that the treatment program can't negotiate around weight issues when the weight loss is potentially life-threatening.

Once weight is restored, treatment focuses on changing the patient's disturbed patterns of behavior and thinking. Therapy is aimed at reducing anxiety about eating, learning new eating habits, and changing the distorted way the person thinks about herself and her body. Frequently, family therapy helps to improve conditions at home—for example, lack of emotional expression and too much emphasis on appearance—that may have contributed to the condition. Patients with anorexia may have turned their home into an arena for constant conflict with other members of the family. Therapy for the parents can help them feel the freedom to set appropriate limits in response to some of their child's extraordinary demands.

Condition: Bulimia Nervosa

Repeated eating binges, followed by attempts to get rid of the food through self-induced vomiting or to "cleanse" the body with diuretics.

Background

Although bulimia is far more common than anorexia nervosa (see above), the existence of this disorder was only "officially" recognized by psychiatrists as recently as the early 1980s. That it was hidden so long can be attributed in part to the fact that the behavior involved with this disorder—the consumption of immense amounts of food, the practice of purging—is usually carried out in private. For many patients, bulimia is their "dirty little secret."

Studies indicate that anywhere from 4 to 14 percent of the college-age female population is bulimic. Almost all bulimics are women, many of whom actually began as self-starvers. The effort to restrict eating completely is very hard to keep up, however, and they eventually learn they can eat without having to keep food in their stomachs. Other women develop the disorder after failing to diet successfully.

Bulimia may be triggered, at least in part, from a defect in the brain messenger system responsible for signaling that enough food has been eaten. Certainly societal pressure to be thin plays a big role as well. A woman who tries to diet to win acceptance may be wreaking havoc on her "set point," the biological thermostat that tries to keep her body weight at a certain level.

Other experts point to abnormal family relationships—for example, one parent forcing the daughter into an alliance against the other—as the source of the bulimic's stress; food becomes her way of coping with emotional turmoil. Because the disorder tends to emerge in late adolescence, it can also be seen as a problem related to making the final transition into adulthood.

The incidence of depression in the families of bulimics is higher than average, suggesting a link between mood disorders and eating disorders. Bulimics are generally impulsive and are susceptible to substance and alcohol abuse.

Symptoms

Consumption of enormous quantities of high-calorie, easy-to-eat foods within a relatively short period of time, at least twice a week for three months; the feeling, during the binge, that one's eating is out of control; extreme efforts to prevent weight gain, such as self-induced vomiting, use of laxatives or strenuous exercise; preoccupation with weight and with how one's body looks.

The effort of eating huge amounts of food and then getting rid of that intake takes it toll. The body is robbed of essential fluids and nutrients, causing electrolyte imbalances that threaten the ability of the muscles—including the heart—to function. The acids in vomit destroy the teeth. Bulimics who abuse ipecac to help induce vomiting are at special risk of sudden death from cardiac failure.

Treatment

Treatment of this disorder initially requires a very careful assessment of the environment in which the patient lives. If there are stresses, efforts should be made to decrease them. The treatment approach should include environmental changes, behavior modification, and family counseling. Some clinicians have had good success with behavior therapy techniques such as aversion therapy and positive reinforcement.

Most bulimics can undertake treatment as outpatients. The first goal is to break the cycle of bingeing and purging. Perhaps the easiest way to do so is to educate the patient about the importance of eating normal-sized meals at regularly spaced intervals in an effort to keep hunger under control. If the patient learns that skipping meals just makes her that much hungrier later, she may develop healthier habits. Keeping a food diary helps.

Another method, known as response prevention, involves having a trained professional observe the woman following a meal to prevent her from being able to vomit. Eventually, the patient learns to accept the feeling of having food in her stomach, which helps reduce the impulse to purge.

Bulimics tend to engage in black-and-white, all-or-nothing patterns of thinking: "If I eat one cookie, I'll lose control and eat the whole box." Cognitive therapy (see Chapter 1) helps the patient examine those thoughts, evaluate them, and replace them with healthier ways of looking at the situation.

Family therapy addresses the domestic issues that may be contributing to the problem. Many patients also benefit from participating in group therapy, in which they share their feelings and learn from others how to cope with their illness. Finally, self-help groups modeled after the Alcoholics Anonymous Twelve Step approach can greatly help the patient with an eating disorder.

Antidepressants can help reduce the frequency of bingeing. Newer medications that help regulate feelings of hunger and fullness by altering brain chemistry seem to help some patients, although such results are still largely experimental.

7

ORGANIC MENTAL DISORDERS

Condition: Organic Mental Disorders
(general information)

This group of disorders includes psychological and behavioral disturbances caused by either temporary or permanent brain dysfunction.

Background

Many conditions can lead to a **temporary** organic mental disorder. A good example is alcohol intoxication, in which too much alcohol disturbs the person's ordinarily good level of brain function and causes unusual behavior (i.e., violence, overemotional reactions, impaired judgment, silliness, or stupor). Other examples are systemic infections, metabolic disorders (such as diabetic coma), liver or kidney disease, vitamin deficiencies, reactions to medications, and drug abuse.

Conditions that may cause **permanent** organic mental disorder include physical trauma to the brain, inoperable brain tumor, and severe stroke.

Symptoms

Delirium, which shortens the attention span and causes disorganized thinking, usually begins suddenly—abruptly—for example, after a seizure or an injury to the head. Other signs of disturbed brain function include semi-consciousness, disorientation (confusion about who and where one is, and what day, month, or year it is), memory deficiencies, and sleep disturbances.

Dementia, often seen in the elderly, involves impaired short-term and long-term memory, impaired judgment, difficulty with abstract thinking, and sometimes personality changes. It interferes with work and social activities.

Treatment

It's important to evaluate organic mental conditions thoroughly, since some reflect life-threatening conditions. Many organic brain syndromes are highly treatable. Treatment, of course, depends on the underlying physical cause.

Condition: Primary Degenerative Dementia of the Alzheimer Type

Background

Although Alzheimer's disease itself is a physical disorder, one of its primary features is serious degenerative dementia. This starts most commonly after age 65, and involves progressive deterioration of mental function.

An estimated 2 to 4 percent of all people over the age of 65 have primary degenerative dementia of the Alzheimer type; the incidence is higher after the age of 75. The disorder, which is slightly more common in women than in men, is inherited as a dominant trait. This means close relatives of people who have the condition are at increased risk for it themselves. People with Down's syndrome are predisposed to develop Alzheimer's disease.

It is noteworthy that elderly people who have a major depressive episode may be **misdiagnosed** as suffering from dementia. In establishing a diagnosis of primary degenerative dementia of the Alzheimer type, it's important to rule out other possible causes of dementia. Besides major depression, the possibilities include stroke, cerebral cancer, Parkinson's disease, thyroid dysfunction, vitamin B_{12} deficiency, subdural hematoma, and chronic drug intoxication.

Symptoms

Early on, the only noticeable mental change may be failing memory. Sometimes this is accompanied by changes in personality such as growing apathy, social withdrawal, and loss of spontaneity. The person may have an occasional irritable outburst, but generally retains normal social behavior and stays well groomed.

In the middle stage the person undergoes very noticeable mental and behavioral changes for the worse, sometimes with depression, delirium, and/or delusions. In the late stage the person is silent, inattentive, and completely incapable of self-care. The time lapse between diagnosis of the disorder and death is usually about five years.

Primary dementia of the Alzheimer type usually involves brain atrophy, which can be seen by CT scan or pneumoencephalography. Changes also occur in brain and nerve cells, but these are typically seen only at autopsy.

Treatment

So far there is no known way to reverse or even arrest the progression of primary dementia of the Alzheimer type. As mental function deteriorates, the emotional and financial burden on the patient's family increases. In most cases full-time custodial care eventually becomes necessary.

Condition: Psychoactive Substance-Induced Organic Mental Disorder

Background

This diagnostic category refers to **brain changes** caused by abuse of alcohol and other drugs. The extensive list of substances which can lead to brain changes includes alcohol, sedatives, tranquilizers, cocaine, hallucinogens, and many others—both illicit and prescribed.

It should be noted that some of these often-abused substances do have legitimate medical uses.

Various urine and blood tests can detect alcohol and drug residues in the body. These are an important aid to diagnosis, since alcohol and drug abusers very commonly deny that they have a problem. Most psychoactive chemicals clear the urine within 48 hours, but in chronic users certain residues may persist for a longer time. If the patient has overdosed and is unconscious, the choice of treatment will depend on test results that show what drug was taken.

A patient who is about to undergo a battery of psychological tests, a dexamethasone suppression test, or thyroid testing should not be under the influence of, or withdrawing from, alcohol or any psychoactive drug. Ideally these tests should be postponed until two weeks after detoxification.

Symptoms

Although alcohol is sold legally, it is an addictive drug and is widely abused. Chronic alcohol abuse—alcoholism—is a potentially fatal disease. Besides intoxication, alcohol abuse can cause withdrawal symptoms (including delirium), hallucinosis, dementia, and alcohol amnestic disorder (memory impairment apparently related to an alcohol-induced thiamine deficiency).

Cocaine or amphetamine abuse can cause death from cardiac arrhythmia, seizures, or paralysis of the breathing mechanism. Cocaine abuse can also cause grandiosity, violent behavior, withdrawal symptoms, delirium, hallucinations, and a delusional syndrome. Withdrawal from cocaine or amphetamines can represent a severe medical crisis, including the risk of suicide.

Contrary to some popularly held beliefs, marijuana abuse may interfere with physical coordination. As with other drugs of abuse, this loss of control may result in severe automobile accidents or other tragedies. Regular marijuana abusers may be lethargic and anhedonic (unable to experience pleasure), and often have trouble with concentration and memory. Hallucinogens such as LSD and mescaline can cause a delusional disorder, hallucinosis, and/or hallucination "flashbacks."

Treatment

These organic mental disorders are part of an alcohol/drug abuse "package" that includes behavioral and physical changes as well as mental symptoms. For any substance abuse problem, the first priority is **detoxification**—ridding the body of the chemical and its residues. Then comes **rehabilitation**—developing the habit of sobriety. Self-help groups such as Alcoholics Anonymous (AA) and Narcotics Anonymous (NA) play an important role in long-term aftercare. Corollary organizations such as Al-Anon help patients' families cope and adjust.

8

ANXIETY DISORDERS

Condition: Panic Disorder

Recurrent and spontaneous attacks of extreme panic that are unexpected and not initially associated with an anxiety-provoking situation.

Background

For many years panic attacks were classified together with other anxiety disorders under the category of "anxiety neurosis." At that time, panic attacks were seen simply as a more intense form of anxiety.

More recently, however, the spontaneous nature of these attacks has differentiated them from other, more chronic, forms of anxiety. In addition, recent discoveries have indicated that panic attack patients suffer from a biological disorder distinct from other forms of anxiety.

The biological basis for panic disorder actually began in the 1940s, when researchers studying why some anxiety patients experienced a worsening of their symptoms following strenuous exercise noted that these patients had higher levels of lactate in their blood than normal individuals. Then, in the 1960s, researchers examined the possibility that lactate itself might be involved in panic by giving sodium lactate infusions to panic patients and non–panic disorder individuals. The result: Panic patients almost always experienced panic attacks following the lactate, but not the normal individuals. Researchers suggested that this difference reflected a biological difference between the panic patients and the non-panic individuals.

Exactly what causes panic attacks is not known. However, some studies have suggested that an area of the brain called the *locus ceruleus* may be involved. The locus ceruleus contains most of the brain's norepinephrine cells. Norepinephrine is the neurotransmitter (or chemical messenger between nerve cells) that many researchers believe is involved in anxiety.

Images of the locus ceruleus area—taken by positron emission tomography (P.E.T.) scans—indicate that panic attack patients have higher levels of activity in this area during normal, everyday situations than do non-panic individuals. This higher activity level in the locus ceruleus may indicate a biological vulnerability or predisposition to panic.

Panic disorder occurs most often in women, age 25 to 44. The number of men diagnosed as having panic disorder may be limited by the fact that panic patients often turn to alcohol or illegal drugs as a means of coping with their anxiety, as they attempt to treat the symptoms themselves.

Symptoms

Symptoms of panic attack may include

- fear that death is approaching
- dizziness
- heart-pounding
- out-of-breath feeling
- perspiration
- shaking
- choking

- rapid heartbeat
- nausea
- fear that one is going crazy
- pain in the chest
- hot flashes or chills

To qualify as a panic disorder, at least four of these symptoms should be present in at least one unexpected attack in a normal or non-anxiety provoking situation. In addition, the DSM-III-R recommends that these attacks should be recurrent (at least four in a four-week period), or one attack should be followed by at least a month-long period of fear of having another attack. Some psychiatrists report that their experience indicates a panic disorder diagnosis can be made without meeting the four attacks in a four-week period or a one-month period of anticipatory fear criteria.

Treatment

Panic disorder treatment has a very high success rate, with reports showing a significant reduction in symptoms in 70 to 90 percent of patients. The most effective treatment appears to be medication, specifically the tricyclic antidepressants (TCAs—see Chapter 3 for more information).

At least six studies have definitely established the ability of the TCA imipramine to treat panic disorder. TCAs other than imipramine have also shown similar success levels.

Some researchers believe that TCAs block panic attack by inhibiting activity in the locus ceruleus, the part of the brain described above.

If side effects to TCAs do appear, they will usually occur within three weeks of starting therapy. Patients receiving imipramine have reported a feeling of being "tense", "jittery", or "spacey". This sensitivity to imipramine occurs in approximately 15 percent of patients. Other patients receiving TCAs may report experiencing a dry mouth, dizziness, or constipation. Often, these side effects subside within a short time. If the side effects persist, or if the patient cannot tolerate the side effects, switching to another TCA, a monamine oxidase inhibitor (MAOI), or alprazolam (Xanax) may be necessary.

Condition: Panic Disorder With Agoraphobia

This is very similar to panic disorder which is described above. The agoraphobic patient with a panic attack experiences a fear of places or circumstances in which the patient feels vulnerable to the attack, or to the personal humiliation that an attack might cause. Because of this fear, patients either avoid public situations entirely or can only tolerate these situations with the presence of a companion.

Background

A recent study of over 18,000 people in five different communities throughout America indicates that agoraphobia is a very common disorder: the incidence of agoraphobia in the general population ranged from 2.5 percent to almost 6 percent. Most experts believe that agoraphobia almost always exists in tandem with panic disorder—although some patients may not remember a specific panic attack that preceded their agoraphobia. Most experts feel that agoraphobia without panic disorder is very rare.

For many years, agoraphobia was seen simply as a fear of "open spaces." In reality, it is not open space that terrifies the agoraphobic, but rather the vulnerability or humiliation that may occur if they panicked in a public situation or place. Common situations that trigger a panic attack in agoraphobics include standing in line, being on a bridge, traveling via public or private transportation, or anything outside of the home.

Agoraphobia is the most severe form of phobia. Like all phobias, the characteristic that differentiates a phobia from a simpler fear is avoidant behavior. When a fear becomes so powerful that the individual avoids any situation or event associated with that fear, then the individual displays the avoidant behavior of a phobia. Agoraphobics may fear even the possibility of a panic attack to the point where they refuse to leave the safety of their home. Other agoraphobics may leave their protected area only when accompanied by a trusted companion or loved one.

The isolated nature of agoraphobia makes the identification of the disorder very difficult and complicates the process of getting the individual into treatment for the disorder.

Symptoms

Panic attack symptoms may be found on page 100.

Agoraphobia's symptoms are:

Mild agoraphobia: The individual practices some avoidant behavior (or endures the situation with difficulty), but manages to live relatively normally (i.e., travels alone, but only when absolutely necessary).

Moderate agoraphobia: The individual's lifestyle is significantly restricted by avoidant behavior; he or she may be able to leave their protected environment, but only for short periods.

Severe agoraphobia: Avoidant behavior results in the individual almost never leaving the home or "safe" environment.

Treatment

Much hope exists for the patients with panic disorder with agoraphobia who do receive treatment. The majority of these patients can be treated successfully. The most beneficial form of treatment appears to be a combination of medication and therapy, such as a tricyclic antidepressant (TCA), with cognitive-behavioral therapy. The medication treats the panic disorder, while the cognitive-behavioral therapy helps the patient to overcome avoidant behavior. (See Chapter 3 for more information on TCAs and panic disorder.)

Most often, the cognitive-behavioral therapy involves exposure-based treatment. In this therapy patients are gradually exposed to their fear. The agoraphobic may begin treatment by looking at a picture of a supermarket, while discussing with the therapist the negative thoughts and reactions that this picture elicits. The therapist will often suggest more positive and constructive thoughts and actions (such as, "You know that really you are not going to die in the supermarket, no one is staring at you. If you can just stay there and not flee, your anxiety will go away"). In later sessions, the agoraphobic may concentrate on leaving the house and only walking to the street. The next session may involve going to the next block, then walking or driving to the supermarket, then entering the supermarket for five minutes only . . . eventually proceeding to the point at which the agoraphobic can enter the supermarket alone for an extended marketing trip.

While cognitive-behavioral therapy can work without medication, many agoraphobics drop out of therapy when they experience a panic attack. Medication usually prevents the panic attacks from occurring (or significantly limits their force), allowing the cognitive-behavioral therapy to proceed.

Condition: Social Phobia

A recurring fear of situations in which the individual fears public scrutiny and possible embarrassment or humiliation. Common social phobias may involve a fear of speaking or eating in public, urinating in public bathrooms, or writing when other people are watching.

Background

Social phobia often coexists with panic disorder and may be complicated by alcoholism or drug abuse. The social phobic person often suffers from anticipatory anxiety—even thinking about a difficult situation (speaking in front of a large group of people) increases this person's anxiety. Sometimes this anticipatory anxiety results in the individual avoiding the situation entirely. In other cases, the social phobic may be caught in a vicious circle: the anxiety the person feels impairs his or her performance in front of others, increasing the person's future anticipatory anxiety and avoidant behavior.

Social phobia, while extremely unpleasant, rarely limits a person's functioning to the same degree as agoraphobia. However, a social phobia may significantly limit a person's personal and professional growth.

Symptoms

The individual experiences nervousness, sweating, rapid heartbeat, palpitations, chest pain or tightness when trying to complete an action (eating, speaking, walking into a crowded room) in public. Often, the person experiences anxiety at even the thought of engaging in these activities. The fear of a social phobia, however, should not be related to the fear of having a panic attack.

Treatment

Cognitive-behavioral therapy, combined with stress reduction techniques, is the most effective form of treatment. The cognitive-behavioral treatment may involve real-life exposure (see the treatment section for panic disorder with agoraphobia on page 103 for more information on exposure therapy) or ''office-based exposure.'' In office-based exposure, the patient, with the aid of a therapist, imagines the anxiety-provoking situation and mentally substitutes constructive responses.

Relaxation techniques, such as deep-breathing exercises, may also help the patient overcome anxiety. If necessary, short-term anti-anxiety medication, such as benzodiazepine (diazepam or alprazolam), may be prescribed. Some physicians also recommend the high-blood-pressure medication propranolol (brand name Inderal) to help cope with the symptoms of anxiety.

Condition: Simple Phobia

A recurrent fear of a specific event or object that does not involve a fear of having a panic attack (as in panic disorder) or the fear of public humiliation (as in social phobia). Common simple phobias include a fear of snakes, dogs, insects, blood, enclosed places, heights, or airplane travel.

Background

Simple phobias are very common, but individuals with simple phobias rarely seek treatment because the phobias seldom significantly interfere with their lives.

Some experts have suggested that simple phobias may reflect an evolutionary origin. According to this theory, the widespread nature of simple phobias may result from their survival benefits. To our ancestors, a fear of snakes, wild animals, heights, water, etcetera, increased their chance of survival. Ancestors without these fears were more likely to perish, but an individual with a social phobia was more likely to survive and pass these fears on to their offspring.

Symptoms

Exposure to the phobic object or event almost always causes a phobic reaction marked by increased anxiety. Sometimes even a photograph of the phobic object will cause anxiety. Symptoms of anxiety include: elevated blood pressure, increased heart rate, sweating, shortness of breath, and shaking.

Often the phobic individual will go to great lengths to avoid the phobic object or situation, or tolerate their phobia only with great difficulty.

Treatment

Similar to treatment of social phobia (see page 105).

Condition: Obsessive Compulsive Disorder

Victims of OCD are plagued by recurrent, persistent, and disturbing thoughts (obsessions) or actions (compulsions) that may be time-consuming and emotionally upsetting. These interfere with everyday life. *Obsessions* often involve repetitive and repulsive thoughts of violence (i.e., killing a loved one). The individual often tries to ignore or block these thoughts. *Compulsions* are repetitive actions done in response to an obsession. Thus the person who is obsessed with contamination by germs or disease may repeatedly wash his hands. OCD victims do not receive any pleasure from their actions, although giving in to their compulsion usually relieves the anxiety that may be caused by their thoughts or attempts at suppressing their OCD disorder. OCD patients usually realize that their obsessions and compulsions are unreasonable.

Background

OCD has traditionally been thought to affect about 0.05 percent of the general population, although more recent surveys claim prevalency rates as high at 2 percent. These figures are compromised, however, by the fact that many OCD patients don't report their symptoms.

Many experts believe that OCD results from biological malfunction in the brain. This biological theory began in the early 1900s, when a viral illness swept across Europe. Victims of the epidemic displayed OCD symptoms. More recent experiments, using sophisticated brain-scanning techniques, have shown that OCD patients exhibit abnormal patterns of energy in the *caudate nucleus*, the part of the human brain that is thought to correspond with the section of the animal brain responsible for instinctive, repetitive behavior, such as grooming and nesting.

Symptoms

The symptoms of OCD may take several forms. Examples include

Washers: These people are preoccupied with avoiding contamination, and may spend hours each day washing themselves. About half of all OCD cases fall into the washer category.

Checkers: In this form of the disorder, patients are driven to perform constant, repetitive checking. For example, a checker plagued by thoughts that his apartment will be robbed may repeatedly check windows and doors to make sure no opening is left unlocked. But no matter how carefully and frequently the checking is done, the checker's doubts are not assuaged, and the checking behavior continues.

Counters: The counter responds to obsessions by compulsively counting objects, or by compulsive repetitive behavior. Individuals with this form of OCD may repeat every action four times: turning the bathroom light on and off four times, brushing their teeth four times, showering four times, etcetera.

Treatment

In general, the most effective psychotherapy has been behavioral therapy, especially in helping patients overcome their compulsive behavior. Procedures that may be used include "flooding"—where patients are encouraged to indulge their compulsion. The patients who normally wash their hands for one hour might be told to wash their hands all day. By having the power to extend their compulsion, patients may realize that they have the power to reduce it. Another procedure involves *response prevention*. In this technique, compulsive handwashers have the means of giving in to their compulsion withdrawn (the handles on the faucet may be removed, or the water flow shut down completely). The patient must tolerate this and experience firsthand that ritual behavior is not necessary.

Until recently, pharmacotherapy did not provide much benefit in treating OCD. Medications relieved some of the anxiety associated with OCD, but had no effect on the actual condition itself.

Recently, a tricyclic antidepressant not widely available in the United States, called clomipramine (brand name Anafranil), has brought renewed possibilities to the pharmacotherapy of OCD. Available in Europe and other countries for many years, clomipramine has not been marketed in this country, except on a "compassionate use" basis in the treatment of OCD. The drug may soon be more widely available in this country for patients with OCD. Studies have shown that clomipramine can significantly reduce obsessions and compulsions in 70 to 80 percent of patients. Another similar antidepressant that may prove effective in treating OCD is fluoxetine (Prozac).

Condition: Posttraumatic Stress Disorder (PTSD)

A condition that arises after a very disturbing event that is not usually experienced by others (i.e., witnessing a catastrophic accident or a murder). Victims of PTSD may reexperience the traumatic event through recurrent dreams or intrusive recollections. In rare instances, victims of PTSD may even act or think as if they are actually reliving the traumatic event.

Background

PTSD was first studied in soldiers suffering from the extreme stresses of war. Over the years, PTSD has been known by other more common names, including "shell shock" and "battle fatigue." The Vietnam war brought PTSD to widespread attention, with stories of Vietnam vets suffering terrifying flashbacks and nightmares of combat. PTSD can strike anyone who witnesses a horrific event, especially traumas of human design (rape, torture, assault, murder, etcetera).

This disorder can strike at any age. In young children, it may begin with realistic dreams of the event. Later the dreams may become nightmares involving monsters, boogey-men, and other terrifying threats. Children with PTSD may repeatedly reenact the traumatic event in their play.

PTSD victims are also likely to be anxious and depressed

enough to receive a diagnosis of an anxiety or depressive disorder. They may also turn to alcohol or substance abuse in vain attempts to cope with the "guilt" of being a survivor.

The emotional turmoil of PTSD can disrupt sufferers' lives on almost every level, from lost self-esteem, to failed marriages, to drug addiction.

Victims of PTSD should not wait for the disorder to dissipate over time—it may only worsen. Instead, they should seek treatment immediately.

Symptoms

There are three main characteristic symptoms of PTSD.

First, the PTSD victim relives the traumatic situation through highly upsetting thoughts or dreams. In rare cases, flashbacks occur, in which the patient momentarily loses contact with reality and behaves as though the trauma is happening again.

Second, the victim may be unable to recall key aspects of the experience, and may refuse to be involved in situations or activities that are reminiscent of the trauma.

Third, the victim may experience a sense of emotional detachment and estrangement from others, losing interest in activities that once gave pleasure. Emotional feelings, especially those of intimacy, tenderness, and sex, can be lost in a pessimistic view of the future.

PTSD patients also experience persistent symptoms of increased anxiety:

- trouble getting to sleep
- lack of concentration
- easily startled
- irritability or fits of temper

Treatment

The treatment of first choice for PTSD is psychotherapy. The objective of treatment is to reduce the patient's anxiety and any feelings of guilt over surviving the trauma. In general, psychotherapy is preferable to treatment with medication.

However, some individuals cannot proceed with psychotherapy because they cannot tolerate the emotions associated with the traumatic event. For these individuals, short-term pharmacotherapy may be required.

Condition: Generalized Anxiety Disorder (GAD)

GAD is defined as the chronic anxiety that occurs over a period of six months or longer. During this time, the individual has been bothered more days than not by unrealistic or excessive worry about two or more situations or events.

Background

For many years, GAD was considered part of the broad category "anxiety neurosis." Recently, psychiatry has differentiated GAD from other anxiety conditions, such as panic disorder.

Although GAD lacks the intense anxiety of a full-blown panic attack, the chronic tension of GAD can become extremely tiring and troublesome. Patients with GAD worry excessively and unnecessarily: a parent may be continually concerned about the well-being of a healthy child; others may worry constantly over money even though their financial situation is sound.

The typical GAD sufferer is a male or female, 20 to 30 years old. Children and adolescents can also suffer from GAD, with symptoms such as excessive worry over school, sports, or social life.

Before making the diagnosis, other conditions such as hyperthyroidism and excessive caffeine consumption should be ruled out, since these conditions can display similar symptoms.

Symptoms

The presence of six or more of the following symptoms may indicate GAD:

- shakiness
- muscle tension or aching
- restlessness
- lack of stamina
- breathless or smothering feelings
- heart thumping or racing
- perspiration or clammy hands
- "cottony" mouth
- dizziness
- upset stomach
- hot flashes or chills
- frequent need to urinate
- difficulty swallowing
- feeling edgy
- startle easily
- lack of concentration
- trouble getting to sleep or staying asleep
- irritability

Treatment

Many psychiatrists recommend psychotherapy that may be combined with short-term pharmacotherapy if necessary. Psychotherapy may be directed to help the patient control the uncomfortable feelings and thoughts that may be causing the anxiety.

If necessary, pharmacotherapy, usually a medication in the benzodiazepine category (see Chapter 3) may be added to augment the psychotherapy. In general, benzodiazepines should not be prescribed for lengthy periods, since these medications can be addictive.

9

MOOD DISORDERS

Condition: Bipolar Disorder

One or more episodes of mania followed by one or more episodes of depression. A manic episode is a period of elevated or irritable mood often accompanied by symptoms such as feelings of heightened self-esteem, little need for sleep, rapid speech, wild ideas, and easy distractibility. A depressive episode is marked by loss of interest or pleasure in activities, often accompanied by symptoms such as changes in appetite, sleep disturbance, decreased energy, and feelings of being worthless.

Background

Sometimes called manic-depressive disorder, bipolar disorder represents conditions at two opposite ends (or poles) of the range of emotions. Most people with bipolar disorder also have periods where they are at neither extreme, but in the middle of the emotional range. The person with bipolar disorder might stay in the middle (or normal) state for years before experiencing either a manic or depressed period. Depressed phases tend to last longer than manic phases. Men experience mania more often than women, while women are more prone to depressed periods. A related condition, called hypomania, has similar symptoms of manic episodes with one important distinction: hypomania rarely interferes with an individual's ability to carry out his usual responsibilities.

Another condition, cyclothymia is closely related to bipolar disorder. In fact, some experts consider cyclothymia to be a mild form of bipolar disorder. Cyclothymia is defined as: chronic mood disruption lasting at least two years (one year in children and adolescents) in which several hypomanic and depressed episodes occur, with any normal period lasting less than two months. The characteristics of cyclothymia are essentially the same as bipolar disorder, except that the individual's ability to function is not impaired to the same degree as in bipolar disorder.

In recent years, research has indicated that many people who suffer from mood disorders have a biochemical imbalance that may be passed on from generation to generation. Perhaps the most dramatic evidence of the biological nature of bipolar disorder comes from studies of identical twins raised apart from each other. After bipolar disorder was diagnosed in one twin, it was discovered in 75 percent of the other twins! This statistic is very significant, especially considering that the overall incidence with manic-depressive disorder in the general population is 0.5 percent.

Symptoms

Manic episode: a period in which mood is consistently either elevated and euphoric, or else irritable. During this period, the following symptoms may occur: overblown sense of self-esteem; scant need for sleep; becoming very talkative; having wild ideas; increased distractibility; increased energy and drive, or becoming physically agitated; increased "fun-seeking."

Depressive episode: a period of feeling down, cut off loss of interest and pleasure for at least two weeks. This depressed mood indicates a departure from the individual's normal functioning levels. During this period, at least five of the following symptoms may occur: depressed mood (or in children and teens, irritability); loss of the ability to feel interest or pleasure; weight loss or weight gain (not from dieting); decrease or increase in appetite; either insomnia or excessive sleepiness; restlessness or unusual slowness; fatigue; undeserved feelings of guilt or worthlessness; loss of powers of thought and concentration, or indecisiveness; persistent thinking about death or suicide.

Treatment

In most individuals, bipolar disorder can be effectively treated by the proper use of medication. Usually the medication of first choice is lithium. Studies have indicated that lithium, when used properly, successfully treats between 70 to 90 percent of bipolar patients. Lithium, however, is not a cure; in many cases a long-term lithium maintenance schedule must be followed. Unfortunately, some patients—having gone an extended period without experiencing any symptoms of their bipolar disorder—neglect to follow their dosing schedule. Studies have found that in the majority of these noncompliant patients, bipolar disorder will resurface.

If lithium therapy fails either partially or completely to produce the expected benefits, other medications may either augment lithium therapy or replace it entirely. These medications may include an antidepressant, or other mood-stabilizing medications such as carbamazepine (Tegretol), clonazepam (Klonopin), or valproic acid (Depakote).

In addition to pharmacotherapy, psychotherapy often proves extremely helpful in helping the patient adjust to life without the wild fluctuations of manic-depressive disorder.

Condition: Major Depression

A single major depressive episode, or several such episodes not preceded by unusual "up" periods (mania or hypomania). If several depressive episodes occur, the condition is called recurrent major depression.

Major depression may be mild, moderate, or severe. It may or may not include delusions or hallucinations.

Background

Roughly twice as common in females as in males, major depression will at some point afflict some 9 to 26 percent of all women and 5 to 12 percent of all men in the United States and Europe. It used to be considered purely an adult's disorder, but recent research has established that many children and adolescents also suffer from major depression.

It is apparently possible to inherit a vulnerability to this condition. Various family studies have shown that close relatives of people with major depression are likely to have the disorder themselves, at a rate 1.5 to 3 times higher than that of the general population.

Although some people have just one episode of major depression and then go back to functioning normally, more than half experience recurrent depressive episodes, either years apart or much more closely spaced. In 20 to 35 percent of cases, there is some residual depression even between episodes. Sometimes recurrent major depression evolves into manic-depressive illness.

Major depression can occur in a person who already has dysthymia (a chronically depressed personality); this combination is often called "double depression."

Even though major depression is common, it is by no means a catch-all diagnosis. "Mimicker" conditions, which look like depression but are caused by something else, often lead to misdiagnosis. For this reason, the initial evaluation should always include a thorough physical exam. Broad categories of depression "mimickers" include alcohol and drug abuse, reactions to prescription medications, glandular disorders (such as thyroid disturbances and diabetes mellitus), central nervous system diseases (including multiple sclerosis and Alzheimer's disease), infections, cancers, nutritional deficiencies, metabolic disorders, reactions to medications, and environmental toxins.

Symptoms

A major depressive episode is present when the first two of the following symptoms, and at least three of the others, appear and last for at least two weeks: depressed mood (or in children and teens, irritable mood) for most of the day, every day; loss of the ability to feel interest in, or derive pleasure from, all or most daily activities; weight loss (not from dieting) or weight gain of more than 5 percent in a month; depressed or unusually increased appetite; inability to sleep or, on the contrary, excessive sleepiness; restlessness or unusual slowness, severe enough to be apparent to other people; tiredness or low energy; feelings of guilt or worthlessness (the guilt may reach delusional proportions); loss of powers of thought, concentration, and decisiveness; persistent thoughts of death or suicide, a suicide plan, or a suicide attempt.

If the person is mourning the death of a loved one, depressed feelings are natural and normal, and the diagnosis of major depression does not apply. However, if the bereaved person is morbidly preoccupied with ideas of personal worthlessness or with thoughts of suicide, or is extremely slowed down and unable to function normally for a considerable length of time, this may be a bereavement complicated by major depression.

If delusions or hallucinations occur, they may fit in with the depressed mood, centering on themes of guilt, worthlessness, pointlessness, illness, death, or merited punishment.

Treatment

A depression caused by an identifiable physical condition, such as one of the "mimickers" mentioned above, may disappear completely when the underlying condition responds to appropriate treatment. If there is no apparent physical cause, a combination of medication and psychotherapy will usually work better than either one alone.

It takes at least three weeks for an antidepressant medication to take full effect. A tricyclic antidepressant such as imipramine (Tofranil) is often the medication of choice. Certain blood and urine tests can help the physician decide which antidepressant to prescribe, and at what dosage. Timing of doses is important: some tricyclics may cause drowsiness, and thus are best taken at bedtime.

Older people, and those who don't respond to a tricyclic, may do better with an antidepressant medication of the monoamine oxidase inhibitor (MAOI) type, such as phenelzine (Nardil).

If medications fail to help and the person is suicidal, electroshock therapy may be justified. This involves low-energy currents directed at the brain, under complete anesthesia, to produce a controlled seizure. It can frequently relieve major depression within a couple of weeks. However, there is a tendency for relapse, which may be high unless follow-up therapy is done.

Even if medications succeed in removing the physical signs of depression such as low energy, poor appetite, and sleep disturbances, an extremely negative, "down" attitude may remain. "Talk therapy" can help the patient deal with emotional issues that may have built up during the depression, and that stand in the way of recovery. Psychotherapeutic approaches to major depression may include cognitive therapy, interpersonal therapy, or a combination of these.

Condition: Dysthymia

Also known as depressive neurosis or depressive personality, dysthymia is a chronic depressed feeling (or irritability, in children and teens) lasting for two years or more (one year or more, in children and teens). There are no delusions or hallucinations. Otherwise, the symptoms are virtually the same as for major depression, except that they are more long-lasting and less severe.

Background

In children, dysthymia affects both sexes equally, but in adults it is more common in females than in males. It usually begins in childhood, the teen years, or early adulthood; it's more common among close relatives of people with major depression than in the general population. Primary dysthymia occurs independent of any other known condition. Secondary dysthymia results from another disorder such as anorexia nervosa, alcohol or drug dependence, rheumatoid arthritis, or anxiety disorder.

Children and adolescents with dysthymia are usually indifferent students, have few friends, and relate poorly to adults. Conditions that may make them prone to dysthymia include attention-deficit hyperactivity disorder, conduct disorder, a severe developmental disorder, mental retardation, and a chaotic or rejecting family.

Dysthymic people are somewhat less impaired, at work and in their relationships with others, than people suffering from a major depressive episode. However, their long-term unhappiness makes them likely to abuse, and become dependent upon, alcohol or drugs.

Sometimes a dysthymic person sinks into a major depressive episode; this combination, which is called "double depression," may require psychiatric hospitalization.

Symptoms

Over a two-year (or for children and teens, one-year) period, depressed mood is present for all or most of the day, more days than not.

Other symptoms associated with depression also occur. These may include eating disturbances (poor appetite and low food intake or, conversely, exaggerated appetite and overeating), sleeping disturbances (insomnia or excessive sleeping), tiredness, lack of energy, feelings of unworthiness, trouble concentrating and making decisions, chronic pessimism, and complaints about vague pains in various parts of the body.

Children with dysthymia who do not actually lose weight

may nevertheless fail to make expected weight gains. They may also be unusually still and inactive.

Treatment

In any dysthymic patient who is taking a prescription medication, an important first step is to find out whether the persistent depressed mood is actually a reaction to the medication. Stopping the medication, or switching to a different one, may produce swift improvement. Elderly people who have accumulated a number of different prescriptions are particularly vulnerable to medication reactions. Remedies that often cause depressive symptoms include certain antihypertensives (blood pressure medicines), sedatives, narcotics, antihistamines, and some psychiatric medications.

If a medication reaction has been ruled out, the dysthymic person may respond to a combination of antidepressant medication and psychotherapy. Electroshock therapy may also be of help. Thus, the treatment is similar to that of major depression.

Medication and psychotherapy may stand a better chance of working if the dysthymic person's life circumstances can be improved first. Examples would be removing a child from an abusive home, or helping an elderly person find her own apartment rather than live with impatient, condescending relatives.

10

SLEEP DISORDERS

Condition: Insomnia Disorders

A sleep disturbance that produces chronic insufficient sleep patterns to a degree that impairs performance.

Background

We all have times when, for one reason or another, we just don't get enough sleep. To be considered and treated as a disorder, however, insomnia must occur at least three times a week for a month or more.

Insomnia can take different forms. Trouble falling asleep, the most common complaint, may arise due to overstimulation or unresolved emotional conflicts. Trouble staying asleep is usually reported by people over the age of 40, especially the elderly. Waking up much too early may be due to depression, use of alcohol, or a disturbance in the body's internal "clock."

In most cases, insomnia results from a combination of psychological, biological, and emotional disturbances. Another factor is lifestyle: too much stress, inadequate diet, and the use of drugs—including caffeine and nicotine—may conspire to rob a person of sleep.

Often, insomnia is a symptom of another problem, not a disorder by itself. For example, it may arise from a physical condition such as arthritis or use of medications, or, more commonly, from a mental disturbance such as anxiety or depression. If so, treatment should be aimed at the specific cause. Just taking a "sleeping pill" won't do anything to resolve a problem with the boss, nor will it cure the snoring or leg twitching which may be the true cause of the sleep disturbance. If a careful evaluation rules out physical or emotional causes, the problem is considered to be primary insomnia.

Complaints about sleep increase with age. Fifteen out of one hundred Americans have been troubled enough by insomnia to seek professional help.

Symptoms

Trouble falling asleep or staying asleep; waking too early and feeling unrested. People often report feeling tense or anxious at bedtime—worrying about their jobs, their health, their relationships. During the day people with insomnia feel sleepy and unrested, and may experience disturbances in mood, memory, and concentration. Disruption in ability to function socially or at work ranges from mild to severe.

Treatment

The first step involves a careful evaluation to identify any underlying cause of sleep disturbance. The approach to treatment then depends on these findings. If arthritic pain keeps the patient awake, then treating the pain will improve sleep. If clinical depression is involved, then treating the depression will help in many ways, including relief of early wakening. It may be necessary to withdraw from use of alcohol or unnecessary medications, including over-the-counter sleep preparations. Behavioral or relaxation therapy help by providing counseling on ways to improve sleep habits.

The temporary use of medications may help by breaking the pattern of insomnia and helping the patient to sleep more normally so that other, long-term therapies may begin. The drugs known as benzodiazepines, such as flurazepam (sold as Dalmane), are often used to help reduce the time needed to fall asleep. Side effects include daytime sedation ("drug hangover"), decreased alertness and diminished concentration, and possible dependence. Any long-term use of drugs should focus on a specific psychiatric condition, such as depression.

Other techniques include stress reduction, supportive therapy, and psychotherapy to improve self-image or interpersonal relationships.

Resistant sleep disorders should be evaluated carefully for underlying causes. There is a relatively new medical specialty focusing on the sleep lab which can provide a sophisticated evaluation and assessment of causes for sleep disorders. Understanding the cause obviously enhances the possibility of correcting the sleep disturbance.

Condition: Hypersomnia Disorders

Characterized by excessive sleepiness during the daytime, or sudden overwhelming attacks of sleep, or extreme difficulty becoming fully awake after rising ("sleep drunkenness"), despite having had sufficient sleep the night before.

Background

We have all experienced times when we drag ourselves through the day, falling asleep at our desks or, even worse, behind the wheel of the car. These periods of somnolence are normal, arising from temporary disruptions in our daily schedules or in our biological clock. But a hypersomnia disorder, by definition, occurs nearly every day for at least a month and impairs the ability to function. Some victims manage to get through their day, but must fight a constant battle to stay awake. Others succumb to the desire to nap.

About 85 percent of hypersomnia cases can be traced to a physical cause. Half of all patients, for example, experience sleep apnea—an interval of obstructed or interrupted breathing, lasting anywhere from a few seconds to over a minute (!), followed by loud gasping, choking, or snoring. The effort to begin breathing again causes the sleeper to waken partially or completely. Some people experience hundreds of apnea episodes a night. This is hardly restful—no wonder they are sleepy during the day! Another 10 percent of cases arise from leg twitching (nocturnal myoclonus). Other causes include depression, emotional frustration, substance or alcohol abuse, lack of exercise, or an organic problem.

Narcolepsy affects people by causing sudden, overwhelming attacks of sleepiness, often triggered by emotional arousal. One out of four hypersomniacs are found to have narcolepsy.

Sleep drunkenness—sometimes described as ''Monday morning every day of the week''—causes a very drawn-out wakeup time, sometimes persisting until the afternoon. Victims, mostly men, stumble around clumsily and find it impossible to make even simple decisions. It's thought that these people may lack adequate supplies of a chemical needed to stimulate the brain's ''wake up'' mechanism.

Symptoms

Unusual sleepiness: ability to fall asleep quickly (less than five minutes) at any time of day, even after a good night's sleep. Also decreased ability to think, impaired motor function, fatigue, depression, abnormally high amounts of sleep.

Sleep attacks: periods of sudden, irresistible sleep.

Sleep drunkenness: need for more time to become fully alert, disorientation, uncoordinated or irregular movements.

Many people with these conditions become demoralized or depressed. Injuries are common, typically from falling asleep while driving.

Treatment

Management of the problem depends on its underlying cause. If sleep apnea (temporary arrest of breathing) is present, treatment options vary. For obese patients, weight loss coupled with supportive therapy has been shown to help, as can learning how to change sleeping position. For others, use of a nasal mask and air pump helps keep breathing passages open. More drastic measures include surgery to insert a breathing tube through the throat, or plastic surgery to reconstruct areas in the mouth, neck, and jaw.

As for narcolepsy, stimulant drugs such as methylphenidate (brand name: Ritalin) or pemoline (Cylert) may counteract drowsiness. Tricyclic antidepressants such as protriptyline (Vivactil) and imipramine (Tofranil) can alleviate the muscle paralysis that sometimes accompanies a sleep attack. Maintaining a regular sleep-wake schedule and arranging periodic naps can help minimize attacks; supportive counseling helps patients cope with the debilitating effects of the disorder.

Condition: Sleep-Wake Schedule Disorders

Sleep disturbance that results when a person's biological "clock" operates on a different cycle than that which governs the external environment.

Background

. Many of our bodily functions, including hunger and the sleep-wake cycle, operate in roughly 24- or 25-hour cycles. Such cycles are known as "circadian rhythms"—circadian means "approximately a day."

Patients with sleep-wake schedule disorders, however, experience abnormal rhythms. For these people, their internal clock may be set to run in 30-hour cycles, or perhaps even 20-hour cycles. Obviously, such an intrinsically out-of-whack schedule can wreak havoc for someone who must maintain a normal life within a society that's based on a 24-hour clock. In other words, it's hard to fall asleep at eleven at night when your circadian rhythm is trying to tell you it's eight in the morning. (Anybody who's experienced jet lag can vouch for this.)

In the advanced type of schedule disorder, the circadian clock runs fast. A person with this condition may feel like turning in at dinnertime, and may be awake by 3 A.M. There's no real problem with this—unless the person has a family, a job, and a social life that are all operating on a different schedule. There's also a delayed type, affecting perhaps 10 percent of insomniacs, where the opposite problem occurs: the person is active in the wee hours, but gets sleepy just when everyone else is leaving for work.

Some people experience random or disorganized disturbances, where there's no predicting what the schedule will be from one day to the next. Similarly, the frequently changing type of disorder arises when the person tries to live according to several different calendars—traveling frequently, holding several jobs, working at erratic times. Victims of prolonged sleep-wake cycles may have a circadian clock that runs in cycles as long as 35 or even 40 hours.

Adolescents are more prone to experience the delayed type of sleep disorder, because of the changes in their circadian rhythms that accompany maturation. The reverse is true in the elderly, whose rhythms shorten with age. The disorganized type of disorder can appear at any age.

Symptoms

Inability to fall asleep when desired; tendency to fall asleep when not desired; problems related to mismatched circadian rhythms such as disorientation, fatigue, and a sick feeling. Complications include accidents, gaps in attention, and an increased risk of physical illnesses such as stomach ulcers.

Treatment

Chronotherapy—time management—helps patients with delayed sleep by showing them how to reset their internal clocks. Patients are told to delay their bedtime by three hours or so per night over a five- or six-day period. Eventually patients "catch up" with their built-in cycles and are able to fall asleep on a more normal schedule.

Similarly, patients with advanced type disorder can systematically restrict the amount of sleep each night in order to lengthen the period of wakefulness before the next sleep period.

Other therapy includes supportive and behavioral counseling or the use of certain medications intended to reset the circadian clock. Care must be taken to distinguish delayed sleep from other disorders, such as insomnia; medications used to induce sleep are inappropriate for a patient whose internal cycles are misaligned.

Parasomnias

Unwanted or abnormal events that occur during sleep. Described below are the three major parasomnias: nightmares, sleep terrors, and sleepwalking. Other types include bruxism (tooth grinding), head banging, sleep epilepsy, sleep paralysis, and sleeptalking. Although bedwetting is a form of parasomnia, it is usually considered to be a problem of elimination rather than a sleep disorder.

People who experience parasomnias complain not about the lack of restful sleep but about the parasomnia itself. In other words, the problem isn't lack of sleep because of bad dreams; the problem is the anxiety the dreams provoke.

Condition: Dream Anxiety Disorder (Nightmares)

Dreams that occur during the rapid eye movement (REM) phase of sleep, lasting about twenty minutes, and provoking such intense anxiety that the sleeper awakens in a state of emotional distress.

Background

The "mare" in nightmare refers not to a horse but to a goblin or evil spirit.

Levels of sleep occur in characteristic patterns. One level is known as REM sleep (a period when the eyes move rapidly behind closed lids). Dreams that occur during REM sleep, including nightmares, are likely to be recalled by the dreamer, often in vivid detail. The content is usually horrific: scenes of falling, persecution, embarrassment, fear, violence, danger, death. Often the same theme recurs in the dreams of a particular individual.

Approximately 5 percent of the adult population currently experiences difficulty with nightmares; another 5 percent have had problems with them in the past. One person in five hundred has them as often as once a week. The "creative types"—painters, musicians, writers—are more prone to nightmares; women are more susceptible than men.

The onset of a problem with nightmares usually occurs early in life; roughly 50 percent of patients who report disturbing dreams have had them since age 10.

In children, nightmares appear to be related to the fears and insecurities of growing up—learning to walk, separation from parents, and so on. Nightmares in adults can be triggered by stress and trauma. Normally, our muscles are paralyzed during dreams; a nightmare can overcome this paralysis and send the dreamer running from the bed in fright.

Symptoms

Frightening, vivid dreams, sometimes recurring, that deal with threats to life, safety, or comfort. These dreams, which cause significant anxiety or sleep disturbance, are not related to some organic cause, such as use of medications. Nightmares usually occur toward the end of the night. A person waking from the dream becomes alert quickly, and can sometimes give a detailed account of the experience. Not surprisingly, it can be difficult for the dreamer to return to sleep.

Treatment

In children, the most important therapy is reassurance. Children believe that their dreams are real; denying the dream—"there's no monster in your closet"—doesn't help. Talking about the dream, encouraging the child to express feelings about it, can help. The presence of nightmares is a normal part of growing up; it does not represent a psychological disturbance. If the problem persists, family counseling may be needed to assure the parents that nothing is deeply wrong. Most children outgrow the nightmare stage.

A technique for adults involves training to awaken themselves whenever signs of a nightmare begin—recurring settings or images of people. Relaxation exercises—getting out of bed, sitting calmly, perhaps writing down the dream—can help. Insight-oriented treatment can help resolve problems of fear, mistrust, or anger. Use of clonazepam (Klonopin) may help restore the muscle-paralyzing mechanism that has somehow been overruled by the nightmare. Depressed individuals with nightmares need special professional attention.

Condition: Sleep Terror Disorder (Night Terrors; Pavor Nocturnus)

Abrupt awakenings from sleep in a state of panic and confusion. The person experiencing sleep terror may recall only fleeting images of a dream, not a complete narrative as in dream anxiety disorder (see above).

Background

Many people experience at least one episode of sleep terror in their lives. However, the disorder—recurrent episodes over a long period of time—affects only between 1 and 4 percent of children, boys more often than girls.

Onset usually begins between ages 4 and 12. If it strikes an adult, it usually does so before the age of 40. Children with sleep terrors are usually psychologically normal, and there is no evidence that a physical problem is responsible. Many adults who develop the condition may have other disorders, such as severe anxiety.

Sleep terrors are very different from nightmares. Nightmares occur during the rapid eye movement (REM) phase of sleep—the dream phase—which reaches a peak sometime after the middle of the sleep period, in the hours before waking. Sleep terrors, in contrast, are not dreams and occur much earlier, during the first part of the night, during one of the non-REM phases.

A nightmare causes much less fear and agitation. Frequently a person having a nightmare wakes with a start, but not with the panicky scream that indicates sleep terror. The person can often recount a nightmare quite clearly either immediately or the following morning, while a night terror produces only fragmentary images and a sense of total fear. Strangely, in the morning, the person doesn't remember a thing.

Sleep scientists, studying the brain waves of people undergoing a sleep terror, have found that just before an episode the waves become much higher than normal. Breathing and heartbeat slow down. When the terror strikes, heart rate increases up to four times its previous rate, and the brain waves resemble those of someone who is awake.

Symptoms

Recurrent episodes of sudden wakening, usually beginning with a scream of panic, and lasting up to ten minutes. Severe anxiety, racing heart, rapid breathing, perspiration, goose pimples, dilated pupils. Often the person can't be comforted by others and may sit in bed, confused, for several minutes while carrying out some repeated movement, such as pulling on the bedsheets, but the feeling of terror eventually passes. In the morning the person has no recall of the episode.

Treatment

No treatment is usually required. In severe cases, such as when sleepwalking or the risk of injury is possible, small doses of benzodiazepines, such as diazepam (brand name: Valium), can be very helpful in reducing or eliminating episodes. However, upon withdrawal from the medication, terrors may return and may be even more severe than before.

Condition: Sleepwalking (Somnambulism)

Repeated episodes of getting out of bed and walking around without realizing it, and with no later memory of having sleepwalked.

Background

About 15 percent of all children sleepwalk at some time. However, no more than 6 percent of children, and less than 1 percent of adults (more men than women) actually have a sleepwalking disorder. Because it is seen more frequently in children, sleepwalking is thought to be connected to the process of growth. A sleepwalking disorder usually begins between the ages of 6 and 12; those with the condition often have relatives who also sleepwalk and who are known to be especially deep sleepers.

Sleepwalkers can move about, dress, eat, even go to the bathroom, but awaken without remembering the event. Sometimes, walkers awaken spontaneously and are disoriented; at other times, they return to their beds and awaken normally in the morning, oblivious to their adventures. In many instances they lie down someplace and awaken in the morning, wondering where they are and how they got there.

Symptoms

Clumsy but apparently purposeful movement; a blank stare; unresponsive to communication; the person can be awakened only with great difficulty. The sleepwalker doesn't remember where he went or what happened on the walk. In most cases the person who is sleepwalking doesn't act frenzied or aggressive. This person may talk incoherently while walking, but engaging in a conversation is rare. Injuries and accidents—occasionally serious—can result from falling downstairs, climbing out windows, even from attempting to drive a car.

Treatment

Sleepwalkers usually outgrow their behavior; drugs are of little value. Psychological counseling or behavior modification may work, but in some patients may provoke unnecessary anxiety. Regular sleep schedules help.

Adults may have an emotional disturbance; benzodiazepines such as diazepam (Valium) and flurazepam (Dalmane) may relieve anxiety. Some patients benefit from use of the antidepressant imipramine (Tofranil) or even hypnotism.

Relatives of a sleepwalker should take precautions: lock doors, hide car keys, and do what they can to protect the person from the potential hazards of his nighttime wanderings.

11

SCHIZOPHRENIA

Schizophrenia is a large group of disorders that involve characteristic disturbances in the following areas: perceptions, feelings, relationship to the external world, sense of self, and psychomotive behavior. Not all the symptoms are found in every case. Moreover, many of the symptoms can be seen in other disorders. The diagnosis of schizophrenia is made only when there are delusions, auditory hallucinations, and/or incoherence, with disturbances in logical thinking and associations. The term "schizophrenia" is used too readily; it should be saved for cases in which the diagnosis is well established. The person with schizophrenia generally shows deterioration in work, interpersonal relationships, and the ability to care for himself. Signs of the illness should be present for at least six months before the diagnosis is made.

Background

The work "schizophrenia" comes from Greek terms meaning "splitting of the mind." The symptoms of schizophrenia were described as long ago as 1400 B.C. For centuries people with the disorder were thought to be possessed by the devil.

Today, it is estimated that 1 percent or more of the population of the United States is schizophrenic. Typically, the disorder strikes during adolescence or early adulthood, but it can also begin in later years. Although men and women are affected equally, symptoms usually appear earlier in men. It's important to note that severe infections, cancer, drug abuse, and even vitamin deficiencies sometimes cause schizophrenia-like symptoms (e.g. delirium, hallucinations, incoherence, absent or inappropriate emotions). Such organic causes for these symptoms must be ruled out before a diagnosis of schizophrenia can be established.

No one knows what causes schizophrenia. Many theories have been proposed, ranging from hereditary damage in the nervous system to overwhelming stress or disturbed family relationships. Studies in twins and in adopted children indicate genetics play a role, but there are many other factors involved as well. None of these theories, however, has accounted for all of the features of the disorder. It's probable that, in many cases, the real cause is a combination of these factors.

Frequently, the first sign of schizophrenia is a gradual deterioration in the person's ability to function, involving withdrawal from other people, odd behavior, and strange ideas or perceptions. The family may notice that their relative is "not the same person." This early phase may continue for years. Following some kind of psychosocial stress, symptoms (see below) develop and become prominent. After this phase, the illness may subside somewhat, but almost never remits entirely.

There are different descriptive categories to schizophrenia; the schizophrenic person may move from one to another category at various times:

Catatonic—This represents a psychomotor problem which can present itself in several ways—stupor, rigidity, agitation, posturing, and negativism. It also may present with rapid changes from one of these symptoms to another.

Disorganized—The person is incoherent and disorganized,

shows "loosening of associations" by which we mean that the thoughts are only loosely associated with one another. This makes ordinary conversation difficult. These patients demonstrate severe disturbances in the usual emotional responses (making no response or responding inappropriately). The severity of this type of illness usually significantly interferes with effective social interactions.

Paranoid—The person is preoccupied with delusions or auditory hallucinations that seem to be organized around a particular theme. Although the patients do not display some of the other more disruptive symptoms of schizophrenia, as described above, they can become very angry, and potentially violent, in response to their delusional ideas.

Residual—The person has come through a catatonic, disorganized, or paranoid stage, but still shows some disturbance including two or more of the following:

- Severe social withdrawal
- Severe difficulty with work, studies, or housekeeping
- Noticeably strange behavior
- Great trouble with personal cleanliness and grooming
- Flat or inappropriate emotions
- A vague, complicated, or wandering style of speaking
- Magical thinking or strange beliefs
- "Perceptions" of people or forces that are invisible to others
- Little interest or drive

Schizophrenia is a tragic and devastating disorder. People with schizophrenia often lose their ability to function on a daily basis, hold a job, maintain relationships with other people, or even keep themselves clean and neat. They often require full-time supervision to see that their survival needs are met, and to keep them from harming themselves or others. Naturally, this can drain the family emotionally as well as financially.

Symptoms

Symptoms are either active (doing something) or negative (failing to do something). Among the active symptoms are:

Auditory hallucinations (the person hears voices that talk about his own behavior or thoughts, or a conversation between different voices); other sensory hallucinations; illusions (misinterpreting evidence of the senses); altered perception of time.

Delusions can take many forms: paranoid delusions (belief that a person or organization is trying to harm the person); delusions of sin or guilt for some misdeed; delusions of jealousy (belief that someone has been unfaithful); somatic delusions (belief that something is happening to the body); grandiose delusions (unrealistic or bizarre beliefs about talents or accomplishments); religious delusions (for example, believing that grapefruits contain the essence of God).

Other cognitive disturbances: illogical thinking, ungrammatical or random speech, making associations between unrelated events or images. Emotional disturbances: inappropriate emotional responses, excessive excitement.

Behavioral disturbances: hyperactivity, violence, repetitive movements, mannerisms such as tics or hand wringing.

Negative symptoms include minimal or nonexistent speech, or speech that communicates very little information; delayed response time; reduced emotional expression; inability to experience pleasure; resistance to instructions; poor hygiene; social withdrawal.

The diagnosis of schizophrenia should not be made until at least one of the following conditions lasts for a week or more:

- Two of the following:
  1. Delusions
  2. Repeated, long-lasting hallucinations
  3. Incoherent, "scrambled" thinking and talking
  4. Catatonia (tendency to stay in a fixed physical position)
  5. Dull or extremely inappropriate emotional state

- Bizarre delusions
- Hallucinations of one or more voices talking about how the person thinks or acts

Treatment

There is no known cure for schizophrenia. Use of neuroleptic medications such as chlorpromazine (Thorazine) or haloperidol (Haldol) reduces psychotic symptoms for 7 out of 10 patients and appears to prevent relapse in most cases. However, these medications can potentially produce serious side effects as described in Chapter 3.

Behavioral therapy can help by modifying behavior through the use of a system of rewards and punishments. In hospitals, a token system, in which the patients earn tokens they can use to buy special foods or access to game rooms, can be effective. This may be structured in the form of a "treatment contract" between the patient and the hospital staff. When well coordinated, structured, and when the staff perform with consistency as outlined in the contract, it can prove to be quite helpful. This system will reinforce positive and desired behavior. Patients can also learn and practice new responses to situations—for example, assertiveness or the ability to listen—through social skills training involving groups of other patients and role-playing techniques. Psychotherapy is frequently enhanced if it is used together with medication.

12

PERSONALITY DISORDERS

Condition: Antisocial Personality Disorder

Deeply ingrained pattern of thinking and behavior marked by conflict with society, incapacity to achieve loyalty to other people or values, callousness, irresponsibility, impulsiveness, and inability to feel guilt or learn from experience or punishment.

Background

More frequently found in urban areas than in the country. Four to seven times more common in boys than in girls. Usually noticed first in early adolescence; peak prevalence is in the age group 24 to 44 years. Even as preadolescents, these children may have been highly impulsive, inattentive in school, and unusually cruel; as they mature they broaden their repertoire of antisocial behavior to include sexual aggression and alcohol or drug abuse. They function poorly as parents, spouses, and coworkers.

Antisocial children often come from emotionally deprived home environments. One of the parents may be antisocial and thus serve as a role model. Most flagrant in the teens and twenties, antisocial activity tends to diminish gradually in the thirties and forties. In many cases it disappears altogether, but it may be replaced by alcoholism, drug dependency, or other psychiatric problems.

Symptoms

In childhood, symptoms include lying, stealing, failing to show up for school, vandalism, fighting, running away from home, and cruelty to people and animals.

In adults, similar patterns persist, and may include failure to meet debts, shirking responsibilities as a parent or an employee, repeated acts of hostility such as ruining property, harassing people, stealing, selling drugs, or playing con games. People with the disorder are often irritable, aggressive, abusive, and promiscuous. They feel no guilt or regret about what they do to others.

People with antisocial personalities typically use alcohol, tobacco, and illicit drugs. They often complain of being tense, depressed, or bored to death.

Treatment

The specific symptoms of this illness make it particularly tough to treat. Patients lack motivation, distrust authorities, and are generally unwilling to comply with a formalized therapeutic plan.

For this reason, group therapy seems to be more likely to work, since it provides an element—peer pressure—not found in the individual approach. Groups that allow confrontation with peers and that operate within a tightly structured community—a hospital or other institution, such as a prison—have provided the best results. These groups help bring home the message that people must take responsibility for their actions and must therefore behave in responsible ways toward others.

Sometimes in these institutional settings a behavioral system of rewards and punishments can reinforce the impact of group therapy. For example, failure to attend a group session can result in denial of access to the game room, and so on.

Once antisocial behavior has been controlled through institutionalization, the patient may find that various talking therapies will lead to an understanding of their feelings of anxiety or depression. Family therapy can help adolescents who continue to be involved with a nuclear family which is contributing to the antisocial behavior.

No medications are known to be effective in the treatment of antisocial disorders.

Condition: Avoidant Personality Disorder

Deeply ingrained pattern of discomfort around other people, fear of criticism, timidity, and lack of willingness to get to know people or engage in social activities.

Background

These people may be temperamentally disposed to react rigidly when faced with anything new. They gradually develop a pattern of fearfully avoiding all people and situations that might cause them any degree of rejection, failure, disappointment, or strong arousal. Skirting risks helps keep anxiety at a manageable level. Behind their self-effacement, however, they harbor strong desires for relationships and challenges.

Many psychiatric patients with various diagnoses have avoidant personalities. Restricting their contacts lets them maintain a feeling of control over their lives.

Symptoms

People with this disorder fit most of the following descriptions: oversensitivity to disapproval; no more than one close friend outside the family; unwilling to get involved with someone unless they are sure they'll be liked; avoiding work or situations that will involve being with other people; avoiding personal contact; deep fear of making a stupid or foolish remark; worry about being embarrassed (blushing, crying, etcetera) in the presence of others; tendency to overestimate the difficulty of doing some small thing that's outside their routine.

Treatment

The basic goal is to help patients confront the things they are afraid of and learn to deal with them at a reasonable pace. One strategy is to apply short-term psychotherapy designed to show a patient how to act. Behavior modification can help desensitize patients and reduce fears about certain social situations. Group therapy can help patients learn and practice social skills with other people. Medications aren't necessary and are often feared by people with this condition.

Condition: Borderline Personality Disorder

A disturbance in thinking and behaving that disrupts relationships with other people and leads to intense, misdirected anger, mood swings, feelings of emptiness, inability to tolerate being alone, and actions that cause harm to oneself or others.

Background

This most common of personality disorders affects 15 to 25 percent of all psychiatric patients. It is seen three times as often in women as in men. Adolescents who are clinging, promiscuous, and prone to abuse alcohol and drugs may be showing early signs of borderline personality. But since some such behavior may be part of normal adolescence, the diagnosis usually is not made until after age 16. Families of borderline patients tend to be either neglectful (failing to provide enough support, attention, and discipline) or overinvolved (resisting or punishing children's efforts to gain independence).

Although some of their disruptive behavior may diminish during the thirties and thereafter, borderline personalities who are still seeking to fill their inner emptiness may eventually turn to sadomasochistic relationships.

Symptoms

People with this disorder fit most of the following descriptions: intense, unstable relationships that swing between idolizing and loathing the other person; impulsiveness in ways that are self-destructive, such as overspending, careless sexual behavior, alcohol and drug abuse, shoplifting, fast driving, or binge eating; sudden, short-lived mood shifts marked by irritability, depression, or anxiety; frequent outbursts of temper, relentless anger, or fistfights; dangerous behavior such as suicide attempts or self-mutilation; uncertainty about identity, as in concern about self-image, sexual preference, career choices, or long-term goals, values, or friends; chronic empty or bored feelings; and frenzied efforts to avoid abandonment, whether real or imaginary.

Treatment

Although long-term psychotherapy can help, the very symptoms of the disorder make it difficult for patients to enter therapy and stay with it. A short-term strategy might help the patient overcome an immediate crisis and indicate to the patient how long-term therapy might be of some value.

Sometimes hospitalization can help by offering patients a clear structure and a strong focus on the problem; it also helps by reducing the chance the patient will act out or cause harm. The staff should be experienced in dealing with the particular symptoms of borderline disorder.

Psychoanalysis is usually not called for, since patients usually need a more tightly structured approach to treatment. Family therapy might be useful if the patient comes from a family that resists separation or is overinvolved emotionally with the patient.

Low doses of neuroleptic drugs can ease symptoms of obsessive thoughts, physical complaints, and the belief that random events have direct personal meaning. Benzodiazepines shouldn't be used, since they can worsen hostility and may trigger impulsive or self-mutilating behavior. Research is under way to determine whether antidepressants or anticonvulsants may play a positive role in the treatment of this disorder.

Condition: Dependent Personality Disorder

A disorder characterized by a long-term pattern of a dependent, submissive attitude, such as turning responsibility for major decisions over to others or subordinating one's own needs to those of others to avoid being rejected or abandoned.

Background

Dependent people stay out of the driver's seat not only to ward off criticism or rejection, but also to bind others to them through feelings of guilt or indebtedness.

The disorder is more common in women than in men. It may show up quite early: dependent behavior at age 6 to 10 is apt to continue into adulthood. Patients with dependent personality may initially seek psychiatric treatment for a disturbance such as severe depression, anxiety, or drug or alcohol abuse.

Symptoms

A person with this disorder fits most of the following descriptions: lacks ability to make everyday ordinary decisions without loads of advice or reassurance from other people; lets someone else make major decisions for himself, such as where to live or work; pretends to agree with others to avoid being rejected; has trouble starting a project or working alone; volunteers for unpleasant tasks to win affection; hates being alone; feels devastated when relationships end; fears being abandoned; is terribly wounded by disapproval.

Treatment

Dynamic and behavioral therapies are especially useful if they focus on the patient's difficulty in making decisions or asserting personal wishes. Even short-term therapy can work. Often a therapist can use the patient's willingness to please to advantage by asking the patient to participate in therapeutic exercises that in real life would provoke overwhelming anxiety. Medications are not indicated, and hospitalization is usually unnecessary.

Condition: Histrionic (or Hysterical) Personality Disorder

A long-standing pattern of exaggerated emotional reactions, instability, excitability, and attention-getting or self-dramatizing behavior.

Background

At the root of histrionic personality is a fear of being found unlovable. Histrionic people pay excessive attention to the impression they are making. They are flirtatious and seductive, but deny that their behavior is sexually motivated. This lets them avoid understanding and taking responsibility for their own opinions about others, which may include deep hostile or erotic feelings.

There are many more histrionic women than men. Their seductive, superficially charming behavior interferes with their ability to function in the role of parent or spouse. A woman whose sense of identity depends on being erotically pleasing may become preoccupied with real or fantasized infidelities.

Symptoms

A person with this disorder fits at least half of the following descriptions: constantly looks for praise or reassurance; acts or looks seductive at inappropriate times; worries excessively about being attractive; exaggerates emotions (hugs strangers passionately, sobs inconsolably over small matters); is prone to tantrums; is unhappy unless the center of attention; emotions are shallow and shift quickly; can't tolerate delay in getting emotional or physical satisfaction; pattern of speech lacks detail or depth.

Treatment

Dynamic therapy seems to be most effective in treating this disorder, regardless of duration or intensity. The goal is to help patients reduce the tendency to overreact emotionally and to show them how to recognize and express their own true feelings and opinions. Because they involve other people, couples therapy and group therapy can help by giving patients the chance to identify and confront their personality traits—for example, their emotional dependency on others.

Hospitalization, behavioral therapy, or medication is usually not indicated for this disorder.

Condition: Narcissistic Personality Disorder

A disorder marked by an inflated sense of self-importance or specialness, preoccupation with fantasies of limitless success, a need for incessant admiration, and relationships marked by exploitation or a lack of feeling for the other person.

Background

Since plenty of evidence from everyday life contradicts the person's inflated opinion of himself, he devotes considerable energy to ignoring or denying this evidence. He can act ruthless toward someone he suspects is more clever or talented than he is—or he may identify completely with that person, taking his or her achievements as complimentary reflections on himself. If the narcissistic individual's bubble does burst, his shame and feelings of failure are intense and debilitating.

In the family background of some of these individuals, these are overly critical parents who nonetheless idealize one of the person's attributes (i.e., talent, good looks, intelligence). Presumably the patient seizes on that attribute and uses it as a shield against feelings of inferiority. Narcissistic personality is rarely diagnosed in adolescence, but is seen in adults of all ages.

Symptoms

A person with this disorder fits most of the following descriptions: feels enraged or humiliated when criticized; takes advantage of other people to achieve personal goals; boasts about achievements or expects special attention for doing even ordinary things; thinks he has unique problems that only "special" people can understand; dwells on fantasies of brilliance, success, or power; feels entitled to special treatment, such as not having to wait in line; fishes for compliments; can't realize how others feel; is preoccupied by envy.

Treatment

An approach using individual psychotherapy seems most suited for this disorder, although experts disagree as to the best strategy to follow. Group therapy, used in support of individual therapy, can help by having the patient interact with others, thus counterbalancing their sense of specialness or entitlement. These patients seldom need to be hospitalized; unless they experience severe depression, medications do not play a role in treatment.

Condition: Obsessive Compulsive Personality Disorder

Extreme perfectionism or rigidity may interfere with ability to function; slavish devotion to rules, lists, and schedules; dwelling on certain thoughts (obsessions), such as the presence of germs in the environment, or acting in certain ways (compulsions), such as washing one's hands many times during the day.

Background

Most theories suggest that this disorder has its roots in parent-child conflicts over authority, autonomy, and control. Roughly 2 to 3 percent of all people have some obsessive-compulsive characteristics. In about three-quarters of them, the dysfunction is severe enough to warrant the personality disorder diagnosis. Slightly more women than men are affected. Neither IQ nor level of education seems to affect the prevalence of the disorder.

Symptoms

A person with this disorder fits most of the following descriptions: is perfectionistic to a degree that keeps goals from being met—for example, worrying so much about spelling and punctuation that a written report is never completed; worries so much about details, organization, or schedules that the point of the activity is lost—for example, overorganizing activities at a picnic so that no one has any fun; insists others do things a certain way or refusing to delegate because others won't meet the person's standards; is overcommitted to work at the expense of leisure or relationships; is so worried about doing things the right way that nothing gets done; is totally rigid when it comes to questions of morals or ethics; expresses affection reluctantly; is stingy; has trouble throwing away worthless items.

Treatment

Dynamic psychotherapy is the preferred method of dealing with obsessive-compulsive individuals, and is usually structured to deal with issues of control and the need for rigid perfectionism. For some people, psychoanalysis may bring about a profound change in their thinking and behavior. Group therapy that uses confrontation to deal with the current situation may help the patient gain a more limited understanding of the disorder while helping relieve symptoms and offering the chance to explore feelings before graduating to another type of treatment.

Behavioral therapy also works by desensitizing patients to the things that trigger their symptoms and by helping them develop aversions to their behavior, especially the slavish devotion to rituals and other compulsive acts.

At this time some newer medications which may be of help are just becoming available.

Condition: Paranoid Personality Disorder

A pattern of thinking and behaving marked by pervasive suspiciousness or mistrust of others, oversensitivity, and a tendency to find evidence that confirms one's prejudices or attitudes; hallucinations and delusions are absent.

Background

More men than women have paranoid personalities. Features of the disorder begin to show up in adolescence. Although paranoid people have interpersonal difficulties with authority figures, and with those who try to get close to them emotionally, they otherwise function acceptably.

Paranoid personalities feel hostility toward others, but they deny this by projecting—that is, claiming that others feel hostile toward *them*. They typically feel unfairly treated, are quick to argue or threaten, and tend to adopt a morally righteous attitude.

Symptoms

A person with this disorder fits most of the following descriptions: needlessly anticipates that other people will harm or exploit him; challenges the loyalty of friends, especially, the fidelity of the sexual partner; reads concealed threats into harmless statements or actions; carries grudges; resists confiding in others; reacts swiftly and angrily to a perceived slight.

Treatment

Psychotherapy that is respectful and nonintrusive, that creates an atmosphere of trust, may be very effective in helping patients deal with the stress and fear that accompany certain circumstances. However, this approach probably doesn't allow for deep insights or long-lasting modifications in personality. Group therapy may cause too much confrontation or emotional involvement to be of any use. Similarly, behavioral therapy may cause a patient to resent or fear being controlled by another individual.

In some cases, low doses of phenothiazines, the antipsychotic drugs that include prochlorperazine (brand name: Compazine) may help to manage anxiety or other specific symptoms. Some patients, however, may fear that use of medications will make them weak and susceptible to control.

Condition: Passive-Aggressive Personality Disorder

A pattern in which aggression—anger or hatred—is expressed indirectly, through passive behavior such as procrastination, intentional inefficiency, or obstruction of progress, springing from one's resentment at being dependent on another individual or organization.

Background

Passive-aggressive behavior is very common wherever there is a social hierarchy of power. The term ''passive-aggressive'' actually originated in military psychiatry.

This disorder is basically an interpersonal dynamic. People react to the passive-aggressive person with frustration and hostility because they realize that he gets secret, sadistic satisfaction from thwarting them. He is unlike the masochistic person, who harms himself to control others or to gain their sympathy. He is also unlike the obsessive-compulsive person, who may seem passive and obstructionistic but who does not frustrate people intentionally.

Symptoms

A person with this disorder fits most of the following descriptions: puts things off; procrastinates; sulks or argues when asked to do something; works incompetently or unnecessarily slowly; claims other people make unreasonable demands; conveniently "forgets" obligations; believes he is doing a better job than others think; rejects or resents suggestions for improvement; won't do his share of the work; criticizes those in authority without real cause.

Treatment

Individual psychotherapy is well suited for the treatment of this disorder. Short-term psychotherapy and group therapy may also help by identifying and assessing the reasons for the patient's behavior. Psychoanalysis may help patients with severe dysfunction. In some cases, behavioral techniques to enhance assertiveness are effective.

Medications are not known to be of benefit, and may even be contraindicated since patients may have a problem complying with the prescription.

Condition: Schizoid Personality Disorder

A disorder marked by a pervasive pattern of indifference to social relationships and a limited range of emotions; people with this condition are usually shy, oversensitive, and withdrawn, reacting to events with detachment and an inability to express their feelings.

Background

About 2 to 3 percent of the population are believed to have schizoid personality; more men than women are affected. Introverted children may be predisposed toward this disorder, which appears very early in life. The schizoid person withdraws defensively from relationships with people because he expects them to be painful. To make up for the lack of contacts, he may develop a very active and gratifying fantasy life.

A few schizoid people go on to develop schizophrenia. Most, however, simply arrange their lives to minimize attachments with other people. They may do well in mechanical or scientific jobs where personal contact is minimal, and as time goes on they may establish a stable network of distant relationships.

Symptoms

A person with this disorder fits most of the following descriptions: does not want or enjoy close relationships, either with friends or family; prefers being alone; appears to have no strong emotions, including anger or happiness; lacks desire for sexual activity; doesn't react to praise or criticism; has no more than one close friend outside of the family; seems aloof, refusing to respond to friendly gestures from others.

Treatment

Patients with this disorder rarely seek treatment on their own. More often they are referred for help by clergymen or other counselors. Actually, any relationship that helps the patient develop an attachment or feelings of trust can only help.

Individual therapy may be of benefit if the approach is friendly, nonintrusive, and respectful. Group therapy is effective if focused on building social skills or helping the patient develop new relationships that can continue outside of the therapeutic setting.

If the patient is anxious, use of tranquilizers for a short

period of time may be called for. Actually, the very act of prescribing medications, and the relationship between the patient and the physician that follows, can lay the groundwork for having the patient successfully enter other types of psychotherapy.

Condition: Schizotypal Personality Disorder

Less severe than schizophrenia, this disorder is marked by various oddities of thinking, acting, or communicating, such as magical thinking (for example, superstition or believing in one's clairvoyance), social isolation, inappropriate emotional reactions, or the strange use of words.

Background

From 2 to 6 percent of all people are schizotypal. This disorder may be a biological "cousin" of schizophrenia. It is thought to be at least partly genetic in origin: a study of schizotypal people who were twins found that 33 percent of the identical co-twins, but only 4 percent of the fraternal co-twins, were also schizotypal.

The schizotypal person may complain often about vague aches and pains that, upon medical examination, seem to have no physical cause. However, his major disabilities are social and vocational. Because of his eccentricities and suspiciousness, he tends to be very much a loner. He may have as much trouble as a schizophrenic patient in landing and holding down a job.

Symptoms

A person with this disorder fits most of the following descriptions: interprets events, song lyrics, etc., as having direct personal meaning; feels extremely anxious about social situations; expresses odd beliefs, such as he or she has a "sixth sense"; reports unusual perceptions or illusions, such as the presence of dead spirits in the room; displays strange behavior, such as talking to oneself, and is untidy in appearance; no more than one close friend outside the family; talks in a way that seems vague or abstract; seems aloof or cold, refusing to respond to people; is highly suspicious of others.

Treatment

Despite their symptoms, patients with this disorder seldom need to be hospitalized. Instead, they may profit more from nonintensive and supportive forms of therapy.

One helpful method is to involve the patient in work programs or other task-oriented group activities. This combination of rehabilitation and behavioral techniques provides the opportunity for the patient to learn and practice new social skills.

Neuroleptic drugs in low doses can relieve such symptoms as anxiety or obsessive thinking, but do little to treat the basic disorder itself.

13

OTHER DISORDERS

Condition: Delusional (Paranoid) Disorder

A disorder characterized by focus on a belief that defies logic or reason, that is maintained for at least a month despite contrary evidence, and that is not shared by other members of the cultural or religious group to which the person belongs.

Background

When most people think of paranoia, they think of someone with a persecution complex: "Everyone's out to get me." Use of the word "delusional" in the name of this disorder helps call attention to the fact that people with this condition may have just about any type of delusion, not just one of persecution or jealousy.

The Greek word paranoia means "a mind beside itself." The word is appropriate. People suffering from the disorder seem to be at war with the world. Lacking trust, they are suspicious and defensive, although their moods and emotional responses are often appropriate to the situation.

These disorders strike relatively late in life; the average

age is between 40 and 55. Probably no more than one person in a thousand—slightly more women than men—suffers from a delusional disorder. The delusions may persist for years, or they may come and go. In some cases, the disorder vanishes completely on its own. People with this condition are usually able to hold down a job, but their social relationships often become disrupted.

It's not certain what causes the disorder, but moving to a new location or country, deafness, or other severe stress may predispose someone to develop it, as may low socioeconomic status or the presence of some other form of personality disorder.

There are several types of this disorder, distinguished by the recurring theme of the delusion.

The persecutory type, the most common variety, involves the patient's feeling that he or she is being mistreated in some way: cheated, harassed, spied upon, followed, or poisoned. Patients with this variety of the disorder often go the police or the courts with their complaints.

In the erotomanic type, the patient believes that someone, typically a person of higher social status, is in love with him.

In the grandiose type, the delusion focuses on an exaggerated sense of self-worth, power, or knowledge, or a special relationship to God or to some famous person. Patients in this category may believe they have invented a perpetual motion machine, or that they are a secret member of the President's staff.

The jealous type involves a delusion that the spouse or mate is being unfaithful. A person with this variety of delusion may look for "evidence" of infidelity, following the partner or attacking the supposed "other lover."

The somatic type fixates on the idea of a physical defect or disease. Such people may believe that their bodies emit a foul odor, or that their skin is crawling with insects, or that a parasite is eating away at them from the inside.

Symptoms

Delusions that are not bizarre but may derive from events that may occur in everyday life, such as being followed, infected, or deceived. Hallucinations are usually not present or are not prominent. Except for delusions the behavior is not obviously odd. Certain symptoms associated with schizophrenia (incoherence, strange or implausible delusions, hearing voices) are not present.

Treatment

In many cases, treatment of a paranoid disorder is more effective if it focuses on helping the patient adjust to the condition rather than trying to eliminate the delusional thinking.

Psychotherapy can be structured to help the patient reveal and examine the complex issues—the fears, the anxiety—that are contributing to the problem. Doing so helps reduce their intensity. These patients commonly deny or distort reality, or interpret other people's motives and actions in light of their own deluded beliefs. Supportive therapy should address these behaviors. Another strategy involves helping the patient to improve relationships that have been damaged because of the disorder and to learn new ways of dealing with the outside world so as to reduce inner tensions.

Although they are classified as psychotic, delusional patients sometimes don't respond to antipsychotic medication. These drugs should be tried, however, if agitation, apprehension, and anxiety become pronounced. Some patients with a hypochondriac psychosis seem to improve with the antipsychotic drug pimozide (brand name: Orap). A combination of antipsychotic and antidepressant therapy may be called for if there are both psychotic and significant depressive symptoms. Lithium, or an anticonvulsant such as carbamazepine (brand name: Tegretol), may also be of some assistance.

Condition: Adjustment Disorder

A reaction to a specific life event that impairs the ability to function at school, on the job, or in relationships with others, usually accompanied by depression and/or anxiety, or both.

Background

Everyone experiences changes, setbacks, or frustrations in life, events that force us to adapt to new situations. For some people, however, the problem of adjustment persists until it begins to interfere with the ability to function. If the problem arises within three months after a stressful event, disrupts life for several months (but less than half a year), and can't be traced to bereavement or another form of mental illness, it is considered to be an adjustment disorder.

In 1967 a study found that nearly one out of four college students who dropped out of college because of psychiatric problems had some kind of adjustment disorder. In fact, this diagnosis was the most common, exceeding even depression in frequency.

Adjustment disorder is characterized by a gradual or sudden change in behavior that can be traced to some kind of disruption. The stressor might occur within the family, such as divorce or relocation; it may be related to life developments, such as leaving home for school or taking a job. Other possible causes include the biological changes of puberty; peer pressure to succeed socially, athletically, or academically; increasing family responsibilities; and so on.

· In adolescents, these disorders often derive from the attempts to define oneself; some experts consider all adjustment problems to be a kind of "identity crisis." Persons with the disorder may withdraw from their previous friends or activities, suffer diminished self-esteem, and feel fatigued or depressed. Many young people may feel pressured to establish sexual relationships for which they are unprepared, leading to guilt and anxiety. Others, anxious about leaving home or making "adult" decisions about career and lifestyle before they are really ready, may suddenly reject parents and their values, leading to defiance, conflict, and antisocial behavior.

Although it is often seen in teenagers, adjustment disorder can begin at any age. As an example, retirement may trigger an adjustment problem.

There are many varieties of adjustment disorders, each with a different set of symptoms (see below).

Symptoms

Adjustment Disorder With:	Symptoms:
Anxious mood	Nervousness, jumpiness, and worry
Depressed mood	Low mood, hopelessness, a tendency to cry often
Disturbance of conduct	Behavior that violates others' rights; truancy, fighting, vandalism, wild driving, ignoring responsibilities
Disturbed emotions & conduct	Combination of mood and behavioral symptoms
Mixed emotional features	Depression combined with anxiety, anger, or other emotions
Physical complaints	Tiredness, headache, backache, pains
Withdrawal	Social isolation but without depression or anxiety
Work inhibition	Decrease in ability to function on the job or at school

Treatment

Short-term supportive therapy, combined with efforts to reduce or eliminate the source of stress, may be all that's needed. Making parents and teachers aware of the problem can help, both by reducing the source of friction and by making adults more aware of the patient's situation.

Group therapy often benefits those adolescents who suffer

from difficulty with interpersonal relationships or who tend
to become withdrawn and isolated. Sometimes, though, a
teenager may look on others in the group as being "sick" or
"crazy" and may suffer a kind of "guilt by association" that
results in a drop in self-esteem or in the sense of adequacy.
Family therapy may be effective.

14

ALCOHOL AND SUBSTANCE ABUSE

Condition: Alcohol Dependence (Alcoholism)

Chronic compulsive drinking, often of larger amounts than the person intended, will cause injury to physical health and interfere with social and economic functioning.

Background

Although alcohol is as much a psychoactive drug as marijuana or cocaine, people think of it as something very different because it is sold legally and advertised heavily. Of the 65 percent of American adults who drink some amount of alcohol, many take fewer than three drinks a week. But 13 percent of adults suffer from alcohol abuse or dependence at some point in their lives.

Alcohol abuse does not present a typical pattern. It may present as a daily problem, only on weekends, or at infrequent intervals. The essential finding is when any episode clearly has interfered with usual levels of functioning. In men, alcoholism begins in the late teens and early twenties; in women it may begin somewhat later in life. Alcoholics have a two to three times higher mortality rate than nonalcoholics.

Children whose parents are heavy drinkers are at risk for becoming heavy drinkers themselves. The vulnerability to alcoholism is thought to be partly genetic. Biological children of alcoholics have increased rates of alcoholism even when reared by adoptive parents who do not drink.

Symptoms

Development of tolerance (needing more alcohol to get the same effect); progression from social drinking to heavier and more frequent drinking, with loss of control over frequency and amount; denial of any drinking problem; blackouts (amnesia for events that occurred during intoxication); anxiety or depression; insomnia.

Family problems; financial problems; frequent job changes; behavior leading to legal problems; car accidents; increased reliance on tranquilizers or other drugs; violent or suicidal behavior.

Digestive problems; signs of poor nutrition; tremor; impotence; high blood pressure; heart problems; enlargement and, eventually, cirrhosis of the liver; withdrawal symptoms including delirium and hallucinations.

Treatment

Detoxification under medical supervision, possibly aided by short-term use of tranquilizing agents. Correction and prevention of nutritional deficiencies and of cirrhosis helps restore the alcoholic's health and helps in long-term treatment.

To discourage further drinking, some physicians may prescribe a short course of disulfiram (Antabuse), a medication that causes uncomfortable symptoms (headache, palpitations, breathing difficulties) if alcohol is taken. This is effective, but dangerous if the patient is unable to understand or comply with instructions.

Group psychotherapy may be extremely helpful, especially in breaking down the denial that so often accompanies alcoholism. Alcoholics Anonymous, an association of recovering alcoholics who give each other companionship and moral support, has helped millions of people.

Condition: Psychoactive Drug Dependence or Addiction

Self-destructive behavior stemming from lack of control over one's use of one or more mood-altering drugs. Drug use continues despite unpleasant social, occupational, psychological, or physical consequences.

Background

In addition to alcohol, which is discussed in a separate section, other frequently abused drugs include marijuana; cocaine and crack; amphetamines; heroin and other opioids; hallucinogens (such as LSD and mescaline); phencyclidine (PCP); inhalants (such as airplane glue); sedatives, and tranquilizers. Many people are also dependent on nicotine.

In most cases of drug dependence, chronic use produces tolerance, and reducing or stopping the drug use causes serious withdrawal symptoms. Smoking or injecting a drug results in rapid, efficient absorption and is likely to produce dependence quickly. Injecting drugs carries the risk of transmitting various infections, including AIDS and hepatitis.

A person may be dependent on several different drugs. Cocaine dependence, for instance, often causes anxiety, so the person uses alcohol, tranquilizers, or heroin to calm down.

Drug dependence is more common in males than in females. Teenagers with drug dependence may suffer from conduct disorder and become school dropouts. Drug-dependent people of all ages are at risk for depression and suicide.

Symptoms

Frequent intoxication producing either euphoria, irritability, or stupor. **With marijuana**: warped sense of time, poor coordination (especially for driving), abandonment of goals. **With cocaine**: suspiciousness, anxiety, or panic; aggressive or violent behavior; grandiosity. **With hallucinogens**: impaired social or occupational functioning, paranoid ideas, fear of going crazy. **With opioids**: lethargy, somnolence, apathy. **With inhalants**: slurred speech, staggering, depressed reflexes.

Lack of control over use of the drug occurs and is sometimes accompanied by a loss of desire to control it; spending much of the day getting the drug (this may include stealing), getting high, and getting over the high; failure to perform normally at work, school, and social functions because of intoxication; withdrawing from family, friends, and usual activities to spend more time on drug use; social, legal, mental, and medical problems made worse by continued drug use; tolerance (needing more drug to get the same effect).

Withdrawal symptoms that may include craving for the drug; nausea and vomiting; feeling sick, weak, or faint; sweating, rapid heartbeat, and palpitations; restlessness, anxiousness, depression, or irritability; pronounced hand, tongue, or eyelid tremor; blurred vision; muscle aches; diarrhea; insomnia; seizures.

Taking the drug throughout the day, beginning soon after awakening, to relieve or prevent withdrawal symptoms.

Treatment

Detoxification to eliminate the drug from the body is essential. Possible use of medications such as antidepressants or anticonvulsants may aid in recovery.

Rehabilitation, with supportive psychotherapy to provide comfort and encouragement, help the patient stay away from sources of the drug, and help manage impulsive behavior.

Membership in a self-help group of former drug users is recommended. Of note: Many recovering drug abusers find that Alcoholics Anonymous meetings help them when Narcotics Anonymous or Drugs Anonymous is not available because many of the principles are the same.

Substance abuse has become a great concern in the workplace. Some treatment programs work closely together with employers in an effort to maintain effective pressure on the recovering patient.

SOURCES

American Psychiatric Association, Diagnostic and Statistical Manual of Mental Disorders, Third Edition Revised, 1987.

Ayd, F. J., Blackwell, B., editors: *Discoveries in Biological Psychiatry*. Philadelphia: J. B. Lippincott, 1970.

Beattie, Melody: *Codependent No More*. New York: Harper/Hazelden, 1987.

Berlant, J., Extein, I., Kirstein, L., editors: *Guide to the New Medicines of the Mind*. Summit, New Jersey: PIA Press, 1988.

Bootzin, R. R., Acocella, J. R.: *Abnormal Psychology: Current Perspectives*, Fifth Edition. New York: Random House, 1988.

Cohen, Alan: *Kids Out of Control*. Summit, New Jersey: PIA Press, 1989.

Gold, Mark, with Boyette, Michael: *Wonder Drugs: How They Work*. New York: Pocket Books, 1987.

Gold, Mark: *The Good News About Depression*. New York: Bantam Books, 1987.

Gold, Mark: *The Good News About Panic, Anxiety, and Phobias*. New York: Villard Books, 1989.

Hendricks, Lorraine: *Kids Who Do/Kids Who Don't*. Summit, New Jersey: PIA Press, 1989.

Masserman, J. H., editor: *Handbook of Psychiatric Therapies*. Grune and Stratton, Inc., 1966.

Mitchell, J. E., editor: *Anorexia Nervosa and Bulimia: Diagnosis and Treatment*. Minneapolis: University of Minnesota Press, 1985.

Nicholi, A., editor: *The New Harvard Guide to Psychiatry*. Cambridge, Massachusetts and London, England: Bellknap Press of Harvard University Press, 1988.

Slaby, Andrew: *Aftershock*. New York: Villard Books, 1989.

Weisberg, L., Greenberg, R.: *When Acting Out Isn't Acting*. Summit, New Jersey: PIA Press, 1988.

INDEX

Adjustment disorder, 157–59

Adolescents
  drug abuse, 26–28
  eating disorders, 29–31
  most common disorders, 25–26
  sleep disorders, 126
  suicide, 31–32

Agoraphobia, with panic disorder, 102–04

Alcoholics Anonymous, 62, 161–62

Alcoholism
  children of alcoholics, 161
  in the elderly, 35–36
  outpatient programs, 60–61
  patterns of abuse, 160

symptoms, 97, 161
treatment, 161–62

Alzheimer's disease. *See* Primary degenerative dementia, Alzheimer type

American Psychiatric Association
  definition of psychotherapy, 15
  guidelines on tardive dyskinesia, 45
  psychiatric diagnosis, 75–76

Amphetamines, 97

Analysis. *See* Psychoanalysis

Anorexia nervosa, 29, 88–90

Antianxiety medications, 45–47

Anticipatory anxiety, 104–05

Antidepressants
major types, 42
to treat major depression, 118
in treatment of bulimia nervosa, 93
see also Tricyclic antidepressants

Antipsychotic medications, 43–45
side effects, 45

Antipsychotics
for delusional disorders, 156

Antisocial personality disorder, 138–40

Anxiety disorder
benzodiazepines in, 46

Attention-deficit hyperactivity disorder (ADHD), 82–84
psychostimulant therapy in, 49, 84

Autistic disorder, 77–80

Avoidant personality disorder, 140–41

Barbiturates, 46

Behavioral therapy, 18–19
in agoraphobia, 103–04
flooding, 108
indications for, 19
in mental retardation, 82

in obsessive compulsive disorders, 108, 148
for schizophrenia patients, 137
to treat social phobias, 105

Benzodiazepines, 45–46
for generalized anxiety disorder, 112
side effects, 123
for treating insomnia, 123

Bipolar disorder, 113–15
psychopharmacology, 47–48

Borderline personality disorder, 141–43

Bulimia nervosa, 29–31, 90–93

Cade, John F., 47

Carbamazepine, 48

Children
antisocial behavior, 138–40
eating disorders, 29–31
gaining self-control, 49, 84
incidence of mental disorders, 24
medication programs, 69–70
most common disorders, 25–26
psychostimulant therapy, 48–50
sleep disorders, 128–29, 130

Chronotherapy, 127

Clinical depression. *See* Unipolar depression

Clomipramine, 109

Cocaine abuse, 97–98, 163

Codependency and enabling, 20–21

Cognitive therapy
for agoraphobia, 103–04
indications for, 22
learning process, 19–21
maladaptive behavior, 19
to treat social phobias, 105

Conduct disorder, 85–86
hospitalization for, 53–54
and suicide, 31–32

Cyclothymia, 114

Dedicated psychiatric evaluation, 55

Delusional (paranoid) disorders, 154–56

Denial
in postponing psychotherapy, 20
in resisting medication, 70

Dependent personality disorder, 143–44

Depression
in the elderly, 33–35
role of neurotransmitters in, 41
and suicide, 31
symptoms, 13
see also Unipolar depression

Detoxification
facilities in hospital, 54–55
in treatment of substance abuse, 98, 161

Diagnostic and Statistical Manual of Mental Disorders, 75

Disruptive disorders, 25–26
low esteem in, 26
see also Attention-deficit hyperactivity disorder; Conduct disorder

Disulfiram, 161

Dopamine in psychotic behavior, 44

Double depression, 116, 119

Dream anxiety disorder, 127–29

Drug abuse
in adolescents, 26–28
hospitalization for, 53
and suicide, 32
symptoms of, 27–28
types of, 26–27
see also Psychoactive drug dependence or addiction; Psychoactive substance-induced organic mental disorder

DSM-III-R. *See* Diagnostic and Statistical Manual

Dynamic therapy
for dependent personalities, 144
for histrionic personalities, 145

Dynamic therapy *cont.*
  for obsessive compulsive
    personalities, 147–148
Dysthymia, 119–20
  in children, 119
  major depression with,
    116

Eating disorders
  body image in, 29
  in children and
    adolescents, 29–31
  hospitalization for, 53
  and mood disorders, 91
  symptoms of, 30–31
  see also Anorexia
    nervosa; Bulimia
Elderly
  caretakers of, 36
  confusion and dementia,
    35–36
  depression in, 33–35
  effect of medications on,
    34, 35–36, 71
  health care trends, 33
  incidence of mental
    disorder, 24
  suicide, 34–35
Electroshock therapy, 34,
  118
Enabling. *See*
  Codependency and
  enabling
Existentialist therapy, 22–
  23

Family
  support groups for, 62–63
  in treatment program, 21

Family therapy, 18
  for adjustment disorders,
    159
  in anorexia nervosa
    treatment, 90
  inpatient facilities for, 57
Freud, Sigmund, 17

Generalized anxiety disorder
  (GAD), 111–12
Group therapy, 18
  for adjustment disorders,
    158–59
  for alcoholics, 161–62
  for antisocial
    personalities, 139
  encounter-group
    techniques, 58, 139
  for obsessive compulsive
    personalities, 147–48

Halfway houses, 59
Hallucinogens, 98, 163
Histrionic personality
  disorder, 144–45
Humanist therapy, 22–23
Hypersomnia disorders,
  123–25
Hypomania, 114
Hysterical personality
  disorder. *See* Histrionic
  personality disorder

Imipramine, 41
  to treat panic disorder,
    101
Inpatient care
  acute care facilities, 52–
    53

of borderline personality patients, 142
detoxification facilities, 54–55
family counseling during, 57
laboratory testing, 55–57
locked door policy, 55
psychiatric evaluation facilities, 54–55
situations requiring, 52–53
see also Halfway houses; Residential treatment centers

Insomnia disorders, 121–23

Laboratory testing, 55–57
Lactate in panic disorder, 100
Learning
cognitive view, 19
humanist-existentialist view, 22
Lithium
for bipolar disorder, 115
for manic depression, 47–48
Locus ceruleus
inhibiting activity in, 101
involvement in panic disorder, 100
LSD. *See* Hallucinogenic drugs

Major depression, 115–18
Manic-depressive disorder. *See* Bipolar disorder
Marijuana, 98, 163

Medical disorders, psychological symptoms, 12, 13–14
Medical mimickers, 14, 116–17
Medications
contraindications, 39
and depression in the elderly, 34
developments in, 6
and disorientation in the elderly, 35, 71
major types, 42
monitoring blood levels, 57
patients' responsibility for, 38–39, 40–41, 70
self-medication, 35, 57
side effects, 40, 70
storage, 40
use of, 7
see also Antidepressants; Psychopharmacology
Mental disorder. *See* Psychiatric disorders
Mental health professionals, 10–11
Mental retardation, 80–82
Misdiagnosis, consequences of, 13
Monoamine oxidase inhibitor (MAOI), 34, 41–43, 118
Mood stabilizers, 47–48

Narcissistic personality disorder, 145–46
Narcolepsy, 124, 125

Neuroleptic drugs
  for borderline
    personalities, 142
  for schizotypal
    personalities, 153
  to treat schizophrenia, 137
Neurology and psychiatry,
    interrelationship, 13, 17
Neurotransmitters
  effect of antipsychotics
    on, 44
  in panic disorder, 100
  role in depression, 41–42
Nightmares. *See* Dream
    anxiety disorder
Night terrors. *See* Sleep
    terror disorder

Obsessive compulsive
    personality disorder,
    107–09, 146–48
Oppositional defiant
    disorder, 87–88
Organic mental disorders,
    94–95
Outpatient care
  day programs, 61
  evening programs, 61

Panic disorder
  with agoraphobia, 102–04
  benzodiazepines in, 46
  biological basis for, 12
  causes of, 99–100
  symptoms, 100–01
  treatment program, 101–
    02
Paranoia. *See* Delusional
    (paranoid) disorders

Paranoid personality
    disorder, 148–49
Parasomnias, 127
Passive aggressive
    personality disorder,
    149–50
Patient-therapist
    relationship, 16, 64–68,
    69
PCP. *See* Phencyclidine
Pellagra, 12
Pervasive developmental
    disorder, 77
Phencyclidine, 27
Phenmothiazines, 149
Posttraumatic stress
    disorder, 109–11
Primary degenerative
    dementia, Alzheimer
    type, 35–36, 95–96
Psychiatric disorders
  of children and
    adolescents, 24, 25–32
  of the elderly, 24, 32–
    33
  environmental factors,
    7
  humanist-existentialist
    view on, 22
  physiological basis for, 5,
    7, 11, 12, 24–25
Psychiatrists
  areas of competence, 10,
    11
  and neurologists, 13, 17
Psychiatry
  advances in, 38–39
  medical basis for, 11–12
  recent advances in, 6

Psychoactive drug dependence or addiction, 162–64
see also Drug abuse; Psychoactive substance-induced organic mental disorder

Psychoactive substance-induced organic mental disorder, 97–98
see also Drug abuse; Psychoactive drug dependence or addiction

Psychoanalysis
definition of, 16–17
indications for, 16
principles, 17
role of psychoanalyst, 16–17
see also Talk therapies

Psychogenic disorders, 12

Psychologist, areas of competence, 10

Psychopharmacology, 38
see also Medications

Psychostimulants, 48–49, 84

Psychotherapy
definition, 15
for delusional disorders, 156
in mental retardation, 82
for paranoid personalities, 149
psychodynamic 17
types of, 15–16
see also Behavioral therapy; Family therapy; Group therapy; Supportive psychotherapy

Psychotic episodes, hospitalization for, 53

Reinforcement, 19

Residential treatment centers, 57–58

Response prevention
in bulimia nervosa, 92
in obsessive compulsive disorder, 108

Schizoid personality disorder, 150–52

Schizophrenia
causes, 134
diagnosis of, 133, 136–37
early history, 133–34
first signs, 134
hospitalization for, 53
-like symptoms, 134
outpatient programs, 61
symptoms, 136–37
treatment program, 137
types of, 134–35

Schizotypal personality disorder, 152–53

Simple phobia, 106

Sleep apnea, 124, 125

Sleep drunkenness, 124

Sleep terror disorder, 129–31

Sleep-wake-schedule disorders, 125–27

Sleepwalking, 131–32
Social phobia, 104–05
Somnambulism. *See*
    Sleepwalking
Suicide
  in the elderly, 34–35
  hospitalization for,
    52
  teenage, 31–32
Support groups, 62–63
  for families, 62
  for former drug users,
    163–64
Supportive psychotherapy,
    17–18
  for adjustment disorders,
    158

Talk therapies, 16
  with children, 69–70
  in treating antisocial
    personalities, 139
  in treatment of major
    depression, 118

Tardive dyskinesia, 44–45
Therapist
  role of, 15
  selection of, 5–6, 23
  see also Patient-therapist
    relationship
Thyroid disorder,
    psychological
    symptoms, 13–14
Toxicology screening, 56–57
Treatment programs
  evaluation of, 64–72
  family concerns, 69
  lack of progress in, 72
  questions to ask about, 60
  resistance to, 4–5, 20–21,
    66, 68
Tricyclic antidepressants,
    34, 41
  side effects, 101
  to treat panic disorder,
    101

Unipolar depression, 41

ABOUT THE AUTHOR

Mark A. Gould, M.D., is the CEO and Medical Director of Brawner Psychiatric Institute in Smyrna, Georgia. He has served in the position of Medical Director for over 20 years. Current clinical appointments include serving as a Clinical Professor in the Department of Psychiatry at the Morehouse School of Medicine in Atlanta, Georgia.

Dr. Gould has represented several national organizations. He is a past President of the National Association of Private Psychiatric Hospitals and a former Chairman of the Accreditation Council for Psychiatric Facilities of the Joint Commission on Accreditation of Hospitals.

He is a graduate of the Tufts University School of Medicine in Boston, Massachusetts, and received his psychiatric training under the sponsorship of the psychiatric departments of Georgetown University and Washington University.